INTO MUSIC

Book 2

PETER BROWN

Senior Music Lecturer
Bedford College of Physical Education

Consultant Editor
James Kirkpatrick

Head of Music
King Edward's School, Witley

Hulton Educational

First published in Great Britain 1983
by Hulton Educational Publications Ltd
Raans Road, Amersham, Bucks HP6 6JJ

Text © *Peter Brown* 1983
Illustrations © *Hulton Educational* 1983

Edited and designed by James Shepherd
Artwork by Philip Schramm

ISBN 0 7175 1098 0

Text phototypeset by Input Typesetting Ltd, London
Music typeset by Halstan & Co. Ltd, Amersham

Printed in Great Britain by The Pitman Press, Bath

Contents

1 THE TOOLS OF THE TRADE

The families of instruments

Musical instruments can be divided into families in several ways. It is possible to group them according to what the player does to start the vibrations. However, it is more usual to put them in these five families:

PERCUSSION INSTRUMENTS are objects that are

(a) Hit

(b) Clashed together

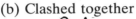

(c) Shaken

(d) Scraped

STRINGED INSTRUMENTS have stretched strings of metal, gut or nylon

(e) Plucked

(f) Stroked by a bow (or plucked)

(g) Strummed or plucked

WOODWIND INSTRUMENTS are tubes of wood, metal or plastic, where the player
(h) Blows onto a sharp edge at the end

(i) Blows across a sharp edge in the side

(j) Applies air pressure to a cane 'reed'

BRASS INSTRUMENTS are tubes of metal, at the end of which the player
(k) Vibrates the lips

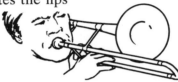

KEYBOARD INSTRUMENTS have the familiar arrangement of keys which mechanically operate

(l) Hammers hitting strings

(m) Quills plucking strings

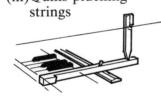

(n) Tangents pressing on strings

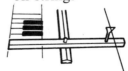

(o) Rows of 'woodwind instruments'

(p) Electronic sound generators

Several percussion instruments are arranged like a keyboard.

Things to do

1. List as many instruments as you can of each type, under (a) to (p).
2. Watch as pupil-players or teacher demonstrate all available instruments, playing in different ways if possible. Discuss:
(a) Why 'stringed', 'woodwind' and 'brass' are misleading names;
(b) in which other family(ies) you could put the piano and organ;
(c) in which family you would put (i) the human voice, (ii) whistling, (iii) comb and paper;
(d) in which families (i) the vibrations can be seen, (ii) the main vibrations occur in the air;
(e) the new group of instruments recently invented.

(a) Listen to a recording demonstrating the different instrumental families.
(b) Listen to pieces written for an ensemble of just one family. Recognise (i) strings, (ii) woodwind, (iii) brass.

In your notebook

(i) (Copy, unjumbling the words)
Cum sail instruments can be divided into five families. *Scrup noise* instruments are hit in some way. *Send grit* instruments have tight strings of metal or gut which are made to *brave* it. *Od window* instruments are tubes which the player has to *bowl* in some way. *Sarbs* instruments require the player to vibrate the *slip*. *Daybroke* instruments have keys which mechanically vibrate strings or air in tubes. A recent invention is the *corn letice* sound generator.

Things to do

3. Sing the following or play on:
Percussion instrument (e.g. glockenspiel) or
Stringed instrument (e.g. violin) or
Woodwind instrument (e.g. recorder, flute):

Later, combine the parts, playing and/or singing. You could also play in succession and experiment with canons from X and other places.

Percussion instruments

These subdivide into pitched and unpitched instruments. You are familiar with many of them.

Pitched (tuned, melodic) percussion

Glockenspiel, metallophone, chime bar, vibraphone
Bars of metal, resting on rubber tubing or grommets. Underneath there is usually a box or individual tubes to 'catch' the vibrations and increase (amplify) the sound. The vibraphone has a fan at the top of each tube to produce a wavering VIBRATO:

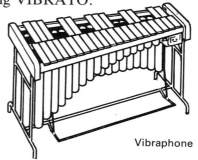

Vibraphone

Xylophone, marimba
Bars of wood, but otherwise similar to the above metal instruments.

Kettledrum(s) or timpano(i)
The only drums that can be tuned to different pitches. The tension of the 'skin' can be changed by various mechanical means.

Small tunable drums are now produced for school use.

Tubular bells
Hanging metal tubes, similar to many door bells.

Unpitched (indefinite pitch, untuned) percussion

Side drum (snare drum)
This has 'snares' of gut or wire stretched across the lower 'skin' to give a snappy sound. It can be played using sticks or wire (rhythm) brushes.

Other drums or tambours
Hit with the hand or a stick. The largest one is called the bass drum.

Bass drum

Tambourine
This need not have a 'skin'. When hit with different parts of the hand, rubbed with a moistened thumb or shaken, the outside jingles add to the sound.

Triangle
A real musical instrument often used in the orchestra—not a toy!

Cymbals
Two may be clashed together or a suspended cymbal may be hit with a stick, beater or wire brush.

Gong or tam tam
These can vary in size, from a dinner gong to the large one used to introduce a well-known company's films.

Gong

Many other instruments are in use, including those associated with Latin-American dances. These include

castanets, maracas, bongos, guiro,

claves, wood block and two-tone block.

Many of our present-day percussion and other instruments originated long ago in the Middle and Far East. Some of these can still be seen in the orchestras of Java and other parts of South-east Asia. These orchestras, called GAMELANS, consist mostly of pitched gongs and other percussion instruments:

(c) Listen to a recording demonstrating the various percussion instruments.
(d) Listen to a recording of (i) a gamelan, (ii) Latin-American music, (iii) modern European music written for a percussion ensemble.

Things to do

4. List the percussion instruments in your room.

5. Look at the picture of a gamelan opposite. What familiar instruments are you reminded of?

6. Each take three bottles and a supply of water. Tap the bottles with a beater and notice what happens to the pitch when water is added. Experiment until you can play the first three notes of 'Three Blind Mice' on your 'bottlephone'. Now compare the tuning as you blow across the top of each bottle.

7. Repeat 6, but this time everybody tuning to the notes C, D and E.

8. Now tune up to five bottles, selecting from pitches C, D, E, G and A. Use one or two beaters and improvise an ostinato against a quadruple-time background. Repeat, each player starting in turn.

9. Play the following, using pairs of notes from your 'bottlephone':

Semiquavers

A new note value can be seen in the next music:

A song from America: **'Jim Along Josie'**

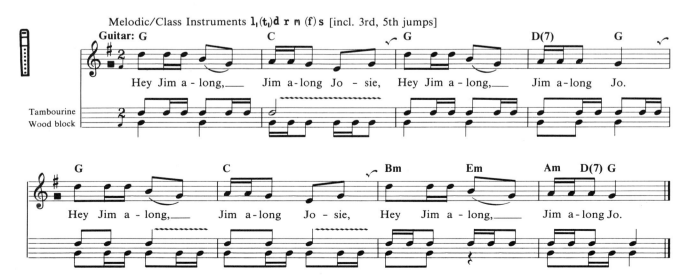

7

Things to do

10. In three groups, simultaneously clap or play on contrasted unpitched percussion (a) the above song's rhythm, (b) quavers, (c) ♩ beats.

This combination occurred in bar 1:

(a) ♬♩♬♩ etc.

(b) ♩ ♩ ♩ etc.

(c) ♩ ♩ etc.

You can see that the new notes, called SEMIQUAVERS:

fit against a quaver:

just as two quavers:

fit against a crotchet:

The note value halving/doubling code is growing:

Single semiquavers have no hands to hold. But they are usually found in groups, with other short notes. Here are two groups from the song:

'long jump-ing'   'scam-per-ing'

The suggested rhythm words can be added to

'crawl' 'walk' 'run-ning'

Things to do

11. All clap a series of 𝅝 counting ♩ beats slowly. Change to ♩, ♩, ♬ and ♬♬ doubling the clapping speed each time. Now clap ♩ , ♬ , and ♬♬ in three groups. The ♩ group start and the others enter in the given order. At a signal, change to the next (or first) value.

12. How many (a) semiquavers in a quaver, (b) semiquavers in a dotted minim, (c) quavers in a dotted crotchet, (d) semiquavers in a dotted crotchet?

13. See who can make the biggest list of words beginning with 'semi'. What should you be able to guess about the semibreve note?

14. How many each of ♬♩ and ♩♬ groups are there in 'Jim Along Josie'? Clap its rhythm while saying the rhythm words 'walk', 'running', 'long jumping' and 'scampering'.

15. Practise the rhythms at the bottom of this page. Later (i) combine, (ii) play in succession as a canon from X, Y, Z, or elsewhere (use any contrasted percussion, omitting the shake if necessary).

16. Practise the parts given with the song. Now a few players add them as an accompaniment as it is sung/played. Finally, add 3 and 9 to the accompaniment.

17. Make up cowboy-type verses to fit the tune. Sing those voted the best at quite a slow tempo. Take turns at improvising different accompaniments. For example:
(a) Using a side drum and rhythm brushes;
(b) A horse 'clip clop' using a wood block or two halves of a coconut hit together.

8

18. Write down rhythms played to you. One of the following will be used, with a ♫, ♩♫ or ♫♩ inserted at each x:

(a) 2/4 ♩ x | ♩ x | x ♫ | ♩ ‖

(b) 3/4 ♩ x | ♩ x | ♫ | ♩ x x | ♩. ‖

In your notebook

(ii) Draw and label four semiquavers, showing how they fit against two quavers and one crotchet.

Assignments

(A) Collect pictures and/or make drawings of percussion instruments to mount in your notebook.

(B) Make your own percussion instruments to be used later. Here are some suggestions:

(i) Sandpaper blocks

(ii) Bamboo scraper

(iii) Jingle stick

(iv) Light bulb maraca

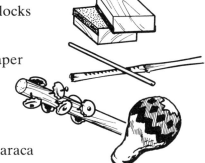

2 A ONE-TRACK MIND

The major scale

Things to do

1. Sing an unaccompanied ascending scale to 'la' from C. What surprising things happened?

Without being told, most people stop at the same point. Did you?

This is because the starting note is automatically taken to be the doh or 'home' note. One stops at the doh an 8ve above because it feels like coming 'home' again. There is no need to count eight notes as the 'family sound' of the next C is easily recognised.

Without being told, most people sing the same kind of scale. Did you?

You should have thought it surprising, because it is possible to sing many other scales or 'tracks' from C:

For example, this one:
or this:
Yet, most people sing this one:

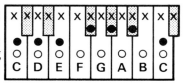

Things to do

2. Listen to the given familiar ○ scale, and then to the X and ● scales all played from middle C. Now sing the X scale to 'la', as it is played. Immediately try to repeat it unaccompanied. Similarly, sing the ● scale. Do you think it is the 'black' notes that make these scales difficult to sing?

3. Now sing an unaccompanied ascending scale from D. Compare what you sang with the 'white' notes played from D to D. Next, watch the piano as the scale you actually sang is played. Now do you think it is the 'black' notes that always make things awkward? Finally, sing 'white' note scales from D, E and F (a) with the piano, (b) unaccompanied. Is this easy to do?

So, there is no question of 'white' notes always being easy to sing, and 'black' ones difficult. It seems that wherever we start singing from, we make our scales sound like the 'white' one from C—unless we try very hard to be different. Why is this scale so special? After all, you never had to be taught how to sing it to solfa.

It does not step to the true 'next-door' note each time like the semi-tone or CHROMATIC SCALE:

Neither does it proceed by intervals of a tone, like the WHOLE TONE SCALE:

Instead, it makes a pattern of tones and semitones:

This familiar-sounding track is called the MAJOR SCALE:

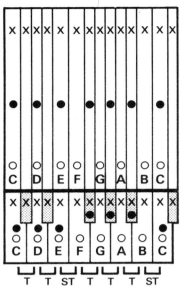

C	D	E	F	G	A	B	C
T	T	ST	T	T	T	ST	

You would have thought that the much neater X or ● pattern would have been the 'normal' sounding scale.

A major scale can start from any 'white' or 'black' note. Each takes its name from its starting point. The above-all 'white' one is therefore called the C major scale. Major scales starting anywhere else need one or more 'black' notes to make the tone/semitone pattern correct.

In your notebook

(i) (Copy, filling in the gaps)
Most people sing _____ scales naturally. A _____ scale may start on any note provided its steps are: tone, tone, semitone, _____, _____, _____, _____. From C, no '_____' notes are needed.

Things to do

4. Hear various 'all white' scales. Identify C major.
5. Repeat 2. Now identify scales starting from different notes as major, chromatic or whole tone.
6.   T   T   S   T   T   T   S
        T   S etc.
Continue the tone/semitone pattern made by the 'white' note scale from D to D under the major scale pattern. As this is played (a) follow your pattern, (b) finger the appropriate white keys on the given keyboard. You can see why it cannot sound like a major scale.

Scales, however, are not tunes. They are only a collection of the notes that a tune may use: Tunes may step one or more notes up or down the scale 'stairway':

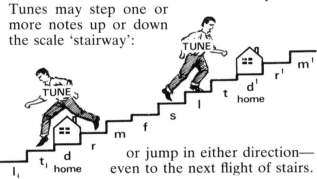

or jump in either direction— even to the next flight of stairs.

Tunes need not always begin on the home note doh, but they nearly always finish on it.

The major scale seems so natural because very many of the tunes you have heard use this type of musical 'stairway'.

Tunes using any particular scale are DIATONIC. They are also said to be in its KEY. For example, tunes using the C major track are in KEY C (MAJOR). All class instruments without 'black' notes are diatonic (in key C).

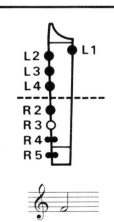

The descant recorder is also diatonic in key C. This next note completes the first octave of the C major scale. You may find moving your RH fingers in one go tricky at first. This RH pattern is called 'forked' or cross-fingering. Notice that you use the expected finger (R2) for F, and then others after a gap. Look at the positioning of the holes and suggest why the fingering is forked.

First practise the scale up and down between the two Cs in one breath. Then practise changing (a) from middle C to your other notes in turn, (b) similarly from upper C. Use your recorder in several following activities, including playing the Purcell tune (page 11) and song (pages 12 and 13).

Things to do

7. With this 'stairway' drawn on the board, sing solfa as you follow a pointer stepping up and down. Seeing the tone and semitone steps should help you sing in tune. The pointer may step both sides of doh. Repeat with different pitches for doh.

8. The opening phrase of 'The First Nowell' includes a complete scale from doh (C) to doh'. Work out its first note from doh. Sing to solfa.

9. Form a 'human glockenspiel tuned to C major. Why are the players illustrated (a) shorter to the right, (b) unevenly spaced?

doh   ray   me fah   so   lah   te doh'

The 'glockenspiel' must now perform as a 'player' points to the notes required for (i) the scale of C major up and down; (ii) the above opening phrase and those of 'Three Blind mice', 'One man went to mow, went to mow a meadow', 'Two lovely black eyes', 'Close your eyes, and I'll kiss you' ('All my loving', Beatles).

Find the correct starting notes and play in the correct rhythm. These openings only move by step. Now complete all the tunes by 'ear'. Beware of the jumps!

10. Repeat 9 with the 'glockenspiel' playing itself without a 'conductor'. Later, change bars but still keep the scale in order.

11. Repeat 9, again with a 'conductor' but with the 'glockenspiel' singing solfa as it plays each note. Next, try singing without playing. Finally sing without a 'conductor'.

12. Conduct these stepping parts on the 'glockenspiel' (a) separately, (b) both simultaneously. Later repeat as in 11.

13. All combine the above, singing (solfa or 'la') and/or playing real class instruments or recorders.

14. Repeat 9, playing real instruments by 'ear'.

15. Try to play 'Rule, Britannia!' beginning on E. Use just the major scale from C to C as before. What makes it impossible?

Modes

Activity 1 may have been less easy in the Middle Ages. The major scale has not always been the normal or fashionable one. In fact, long ago it was considered too jolly a musical 'stairway' (even wicked!) for respectable tunes. One of the reasons why much really old music sounds strange is that the tunes use unfamiliar 'tracks'. The same goes for much African and Oriental music—like that of the gamelan. Tunes always take on the 'flavour' of the scale they use.

Right up to the time of Elizabeth I, composers used white note scales or MODES starting from any note—not just C. It was not until Purcell's time that the major scale preference began. The MODAL SCALES starting from other notes then went out of fashion. Although many composers are now experimenting with different 'tracks', the major scale is still in fashion for much music, including 'pop'.

(a) Listen to music of all periods and from different parts of the world. Discuss (i) whether the tunes use major scales or other 'tracks', (ii) whether or not the music is European.

(b) Before listening to the following major scale rondeau (dance), clap its rhythm. As the extract keeps returning, trace the notes with a finger each time.

Main theme of the Rondeau from the *Fairy Queen*   **Purcell**

Melodic Instruments

A modal sea shanty: 'What shall we do with the Drunken Sailor?'

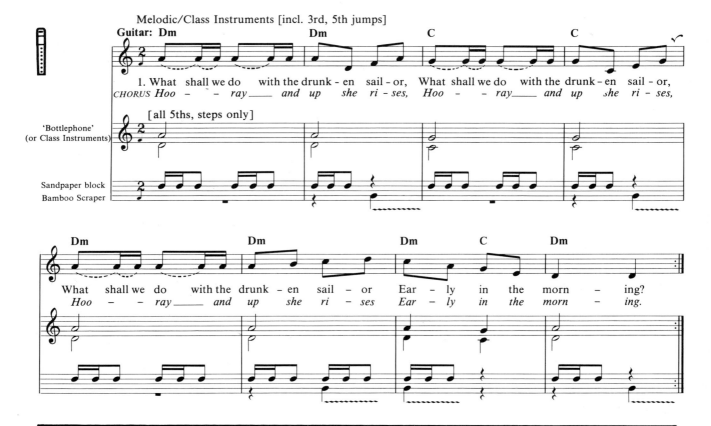

Things to do

16. Practise/perform the above two pieces. Both sing and play the song. Identify (a) each 3rd and 5th jump in the song, (b) other jumps in the Purcell extract.

17. Make up further verses. Perform the best.

18. Repeat 15 and 16 of Chapter 1, using sandpaper blocks for one of the parts.

19. The above song uses the D to D white note modal scale. Immediately after singing it, try to sing (a) this particular mode, (b) the D major scale. Discuss odd things that might have happened.

20. First listen to the scale of D major and then to the above song changed to fit the major scale 'stairway'. Now sing it in this variation.

21. Identify familiar tunes made to fit the wrong stairway. Try singing them with the piano.

22. Sing a major scale to solfa from doh, but stop at te. Discuss the effect of this. The illustration on page 10 might help you.

Some musical intervals behave rather like magnets. The closer notes are, the stronger the magnetic pull one way or the other. The strongest musical attraction is across the semitone gap between te and doh. This means that in many tunes (as in some homes):

after t(ea) comes d(inner)

Things to do

23. In two groups, sing (a) doh doh/doh ray, (b) doh doh/doh te, holding on the different notes against each other. Which mixture is (i) the harsher, (ii) the semitone?

24. Make another 'human glockenspiel'. This time, omit fah (F) and te (B), but still leave room for them.

Take turns at 'playing it' by pointing to any notes in the rhythm of (a) 'Three Blind Mice', (b) 'Jingle Bells'. Although notes may be repeated or jump anyhow, always end on doh (C).

25. Now make two 'glockenspiels' as above. Under two conductors and at the same tempo, combine improvised tunes using both rhythms.

26. Repeat 24 and 25, (a) singing solfa as you play your chime bar, (b) just singing.

A major scale without its 4th (fah) and 7th (te) notes is called a PENTATONIC SCALE.

As there are no semitones between any of the five notes that are left:
(a) There are no strong 'magnetic' pulls between notes. Pentatonic tunes can therefore jump anywhere without sounding too awkward.
(b) No really harsh mixtures are possible. Pentatonic tunes will usually combine pleasantly.

When you use instruments for pentatonic playing, subtract the unwanted bars if you can: e.g.

track is now prepared for these tunes:

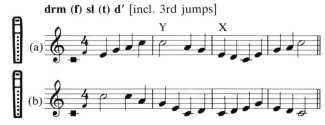

Later combine or sing in succession as a round from X or Y. Repeat, using class instruments and/or recorders.

Both 'Jim Along Josie' on page 7 and the following song have pentatonic tunes. We can therefore play around with them in various ways—but they must be put in the same key!

They may be performed simultaneously as a QUODLIBET. Either song may be performed simultaneously with itself—at half the speed, called AUGMENTATION (notes twice as long) or at twice the speed, called DIMINUTION (notes half as long).

Things to do

27. Repeat previous activities with the 'conductor' actually playing a class instrument as above.

28. In two groups, combine   d r m f s l t d'
                              d r m( )s l( )d'
Change parts. Now all sing the second (pentatonic) scale imagining the missing notes. The

An American singing game: 'Turn the Glasses Over'

A change of key for: 'Jim Along Josie'

Things to do

29. In two groups, sing 'Turn the Glasses Over' and 'Jim Along Josie' as a quodlibet, repeating the second one as necessary. Later, add class instrument/recorder ostinati using any one- or two-bar phrases from either tune.

30. Here are the beginnings of each tune written in diminution and augmentation respectively. Continue each one to X on manuscript paper.

31. Mix normal and varied versions of both songs simultaneously (singing/playing).

32. Sing or play 'Jim Along Josie' first as on page 7, and then page 13. Discuss (a) whether the key changes higher or lower, (b) whether changing the key also changes the tune/intervals, (c) other musical and non-musical meanings of 'key'. Repeat, singing to solfa.

33. Write down phrases played to you in this rhythm:

The notes used will be those in 30(b). The starting note will be given.

In your notebook

(ii) (Copy, unjumbling the words)
Nutes using the C major scale are in *yek* C. Any tune can be put into a higher or *relow* key. The other all-'white' note scales are called *domes*. *Open intact* scales have just five notes.

(iii) Describe the following in your own words: (a) quodlibet, (b) augmentation, (c) diminution.

(iv) Copy/colour the tune 'stairway' on page 10.

3 SOUNDS INTERESTING

Music without scales or beats

If you have a 'one-track mind' it is difficult to think of anything else. You have already discovered that music using unusual scales can sound strange. Some modern composers use no real scale at all. This can make their music very difficult to understand, especially when they also do away with a regular beat, use an experimental code—or even leave many things to chance. In their search for new 'sounds interesting' some composers now use unusual instruments and experiment with unusual ways of using normal ones or voices.

 (a) Listen to modern experimental music. Discuss whether the composer has done without a normal scale or beat, or has experimented in some other way.

Now it is your turn to experiment.

Things to do

1. Place four or five 'black' or 'white' chime bars in pitch or random order. Take turns at playing any notes in the rhythm of a simple song like those in 2. See who can recognise the song first. Now try playing the same tune twice!

2. Choose one of these song rhythms to play as in 1:
'Three Blind Mice'   'Ten Green Bottles'
'Twinkle Twinkle Little Star'   'Jingle Bells'
First, all play simultaneously against a duple beat. Then combine in groups of four: (a) starting together, (b) starting when you like. Identify who plays each rhythm. Can you still do this if each plays at a different tempo?

3. Get into groups of four, each pupil with two or more random chime bars. One pupil play an ostinato on any notes and in any rhythm. The others then add their own ostinato in turn, trying not to copy the rhythm of the previous player(s). Take turns at playing to the class.

4. Repeat 3, playing the notes of each ostinato in the same order, but in a different rhythm at each repetition, and with no regular beat. Do not all start together and introduce varying time gaps between the repetitions.

14

In the last experiments you did away with proper scales and a regular beat. Now prepare to do without proper instruments. Assemble any home-made instruments (Chapter 1) and objects capable of making interesting pitched or unpitched sounds. Here are some ideas:

Things to do

5. Experiment with ways of obtaining sounds from the objects you have brought. If they have to be hit, try different beaters and damping methods.

6. Each take a musical object and decide on an order of playing. The first pupil make regular sounds at a slow tempo. The next one add regular or irregular sounds to make the combined pattern interesting. The other pupils then similarly start in turn. Try not to copy anybody else.

7. Get into small groups, each pupil with a musical object to play. Experiment with interesting combinations of sound patterns.

8. Pass a chain of sounds round the class. Next, (a) reverse the order, (b) decide on an order unrelated to seating position, (c) wait for fading sounds to finish before playing.

Later, repeat any of the above, trying to deceive the previous player by playing the object in different ways. For example, you could play softer, make more sounds, use another beater or damp differently or sooner.

9. Divide into two groups using contrasted objects. For example, pitched/unpitched, metal/wood, short sounds/long sounds. At a signal, the first group play one sound. The second group listen very carefully and each play when the last sound has died away. The first group then similarly plays, and so on. Repeat with eyes closed so that full attention can be given

to waiting for absolute silence before playing. Finally, introduce the counting of, say, five seconds of silence between each group's playing.

10. Choose one of the following sound patterns to play. It must suit your musical object. Do not necessarily start together:

(a) Ten sounds at a fast tempo; soft, getting louder. Wait five seconds then repeat.
(b) Irregular short sounds, starting loud and gradually getting softer until inaudible.
(c) A group of three regular long sounds played soft–loud–soft. Repeat after twenty seconds.
(d) Soft sounds getting faster. Stop when the limit reached.
(e) The rhythm of your names played four times at irregular intervals.
(f) Choose another pupil and play one loud short sound every time that person plays.
(g) Five short bursts of sounds, each separated by about six seconds.

Sequence and modulation

Things to do

11. The next song brings us back to major scale (key) music. After hearing it played, discuss what 'Sounds Interesting' between bars 21 and 36.

In 'Dry Bones', a two-bar phrase (bars 21/2) is immediately repeated seven times, a step higher each time. Shortly afterwards, the process is reversed. Music repeated more or less exactly at any higher or lower pitch is called SEQUENTIAL. As phrases do not sound different in a SEQUENCE, it is fun being able to guess how each repetition is going to sound before it happens. In the above case, as each repetition is exactly a semitone higher or lower each time, each one must also be in a different major key. So, although the song starts in key C, from bar 21 it moves its home note (doh) every two bars. Here are all the home notes used:

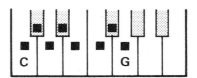

A spiritual from America: 'Dry Bones'

16

Any change of key, whether in a sequence or not, is called a MODULATION. Remember, when doh changes, all the other notes of the scale must go up or down with it. It is quite normal for most music to change key. However, it is unusual for a short piece to change key as often and as suddenly as this. How would you like to move home every day!

Sequences need not change key or be exact repetitions.

Things to do

12. Listen to the descending sequence of the song played on the piano. Do you get a 'sinking' feeling? Why does it suit the words so well? Now listen to it played again, but continuing further by semitones into even lower keys. Can you guess what each new phrase is going to sound like? Repeat, singing 'la' with the piano. Finally, turn to page 11 and find one- and two-bar sequences in the Purcell extract.

13. Listen to simple tunes like 'Happy Birthday to You' played in different keys. Notice that the tune never really changes. Can you recognise when the original key version is played?

14. In groups, work out percussion accompaniments to match the words of 'Dry Bones'. Use suitable musical objects, home-made instruments and any xylophones or wood blocks. Take turns at accompanying a group singing the song. Vote for the best 'word painting'.

15. Sing the song accompanied by the winning group of 14. Add a glockenspiel during the sequences, playing C where indicated above the music and rising a semitone every two bars up to G. Later, descend from G back to C. Any recorder players could practise their low notes by playing the sections in key C before and after these sequences.

In your notebook

(i) (Copy, unjumbling the words)
I scum does not usually stay long in any one key. It often has at least one change of key or *moan it loud*. When the same phrase is repeated higher or lower it is called a *queen sec*.

Changing key or the home note can be disturbing if it happens too often or too suddenly. Having no 'home' at all can be even more disturbing. This is another reason why music not using a proper scale sounds so unusual.

Now prepare for some more 'homeless' music experiments. Assemble not only musical objects and home-made instruments but also all available class and pupil instruments. Most proper instruments have easily-damaged parts and all need very delicate handling. However, with care they may also be played in unusual ways:

Contrasting sounds

You are often asked to use contrasting instruments or sounds. Here are some divisions.

percussion/stringed/woodwind/brass/keyboard
orchestral/classroom/home-made/objects
pitched/unpitched
hit/not hit
blown/not blown
metal/wood
large/small
chromatic/diatonic
'white' notes/'black' notes
high pitch/low pitch
sustained sounds/fading sounds/short sounds
loud sounds/soft sounds only
lessons required/no lessons required

Things to do

16. Suggest other contrasting categories to add to the list. Now write down the musical object(s)/home-made or private instrument(s) you have brought. Describe each one by listing as many of the above words that seem appropriate.

17. Experiment with ways of obtaining interesting new sounds. Play orchestral/class instruments in unusual ways. But be careful!
18. Have a sound quiz. With eyes closed, identify instruments played in unusual ways.

19. Repeat 6 to 10, using any instruments (played normally or otherwise) as well as musical objects. When necessary, contrast them in some of the ways suggested above.

Here are some more code symbols. First, those that refer to contrasts in volume — or DYNAMICS, used in all types of music:

mf   moderately loudly (the Italian for this is *mezzo forte*—pronounced 'metso fortay').

mp   moderately softly (*mezzo piano*—pronounced 'metso peearno').

ff   very loudly (*fortissimo*).

pp   very softly (*pianissimo*).

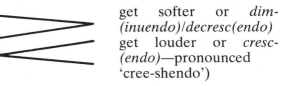

get softer or *dim-(inuendo)/decresc(endo)*
get louder or *cresc-(endo)*—pronounced 'cree-shendo')

Now here are two that tell you to play in a special way:

A very quick slide up or down a pitched instrument, a GLISSANDO.

A sustained non-fading note on a suitable instrument.

In the following, contrast the instruments/objects used by each player/group in different ways. Include both normal and unusual ways of playing them.

Things to do

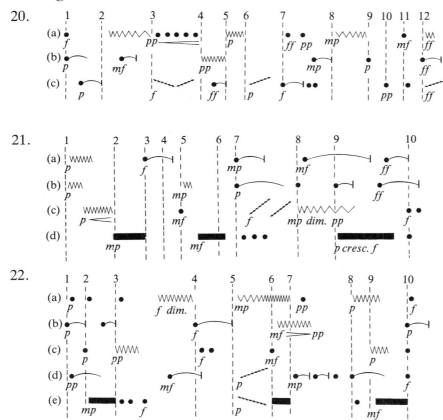

18

23. Copy the following grid:

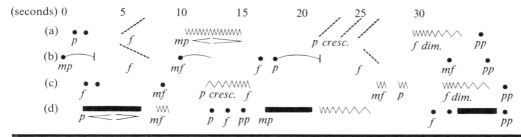

Each choose an instrument/object to play and write a part for it. Add dynamics. All play together under a conductor. With a large class you may find your grids are too full! Later, play each other's parts.

24. In groups, compose a grid for your number of players minus one. Choose a conductor and play to the class.

25. Again copy the grid as in 23. Add the code symbols as sounds are played to you by a conductor also counting the grid numbers. Add the dynamics during a second playing.

26. No conductor is needed for this:

---

4   CAN YOU BEAT IT!

American note names

American name		English name
whole note	o	semibreve
half note	𝅗𝅥	minim
quarter note	𝅘𝅥	crotchet
eighth note	𝅘𝅥𝅮	quaver
sixteenth note (and so on)	𝅘𝅥𝅯	semiquaver

Not all countries use our funny note value names of crotchet, quaver, etc. North America and parts of Europe use a much more sensible system, as shown opposite.

American note names also help us to write time signatures properly. Remember:

The number of beats in the bar is given by the upper figure e.g.:

Underneath has been shown the note value to be used as the beat, e.g:

Using its American name, $\frac{2}{\text{𝅘𝅥}}$ can now become $\frac{2}{4}$ two quarter notes in a bar

Similarly, $\frac{3}{\text{𝅘𝅥}}$ becomes $\frac{3}{4}$ three quarter notes in a bar

And $\frac{4}{\text{𝅘𝅥}}$ becomes $\frac{4}{4}$ four quarter notes in a bar

⅜. is less easy to change.

As a ♩. is equal to three ♪ (eighth) notes

⅜. ought to be **²⅜** two (lots of) three-eighth notes

Instead, the total of eighth notes is shown:

♫♫ ♫♫   **⁶⁄₈** six eighth notes

Similarly, **⅜.** becomes **⁹⁄₈** nine eighth notes in a bar

And **⁴⁄₈.** becomes **¹²⁄₈** twelve eighth notes in a bar

   Later, you will see that other note values are sometimes used as the beat note. Unless the time changes, a time signature is only written once at the beginning of the first line.

In your notebook

(i) Copy the given note value chart, using both the American and English names.

(ii) Explain why **³** is written as **¾** .

Rhythm shorthand

When writing just the rhythm, time can be saved by leaving out the black note heads:

Things to do

1. Recognise a series of ○ , ♩ , ⊓ or ⊓⊓ played in alternation with a ♩ beat.
2. The given note value chart can be continued. Draw and give the American name of the next (shorter) note in the system. There was once a note twice as long as a semibreve. Write what you think it is called in both systems.
3. Write out the above two-bar phrase using proper note symbols.
4. Copy the following using 'shorthand', adding the correct time signature to each bar:

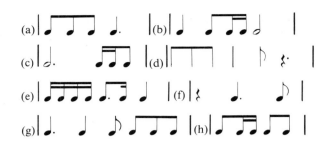

Later, clap (a)-(d) as ostinati. Now discuss (i) the ways a time signature is/is not like an arithmetic fraction, (ii) whether its upper figure indicates the number of notes in a bar.
5. Now copy phrases (a) to (e), completing the bar lines. As (f), compose your own four-bar phrase in duple time.

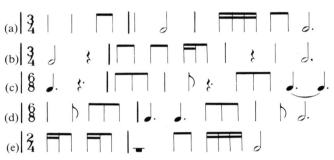

6. As quarter notes are also usually one-beat notes, the American name system can seem a little confusing. However, it has great advantages. Discuss what they might be.
7. How many:
(a) Sixteenth notes in a whole note?
(b) Eighth notes in a half note?
(c) Sixteenth notes in a minim?

(d) ♪ in a whole note?
(e) Semiquavers in a dotted quarter note?

Beating time

(a) Listen to short musical extracts. Silently tap the regular beats. Count 'one' on each accent and so work out the time. Then let the faster notes help you identify ♩ or ♩. beats. Write the time signature of each.

Counting beat numbers is useful for working out the time of music when listening or playing. But you can hardly expect conductors to shout

20

out the beat numbers to keep their orchestra or choir in time together.

Conductors therefore BEAT TIME that can be seen by the players or singers. Here are the basic arm movements of beating time or CONDUCTING:

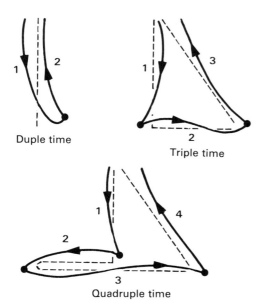

Duple time

Triple time

Quadruple time

Although most conductors vary these movements a great deal, the stronger first beat is always the stronger downwards movement. Energetic music in particular requires a little wrist 'click' or bounce at the end of each stroke to show the beat's exact position.

Things to do

8. Practise beating the above times in turn.
9. Choose two pupils to beat e.g. duple time at the same tempo. See how long they stay in time together with their eyes shut. Use a pendulum as the standard. Repeat, changing its length (tempo). Find the champion conductor.
10. Divide into two groups. Face each other, one beating triple time and the other quadruple. Put each other off by exaggerating the strong downbeats or by counting the beat numbers as well (at the same tempo).
11. Repeat some previous activities where counting can be replaced by following a conductor. Also, beat time while singing songs.

 (b) Listen to more music of any type. First work out the time of each piece by making a downbeat stroke with each strong beat and fitting in

the correct number of other strokes between them. Now all beat time together as each piece is played again. Beat more jerkily (with stronger 'clicks') or more smoothly according to the style of the music. Discuss the movements of any conductors you have seen on television or at a concert.

Later, just for fun, beat the wrong time as a piece is played. Do the first beats ever come right?

(c) Repeat (b) but now work out the times secretly by making very small finger or hand movements. Write down the time signature after each piece.

In your notebook

(iii) Copy and label the above beating time diagrams.

Semiquavers

The following song includes four different beat groups including sixteenth notes (semiquavers). Two of them we have already fitted rhythm words to:

'long jump-ing',   'scam-per-ing'

Here are the other two, with their suggested rhythm words:

'su-per-son-ic'   'hurd-ling'

Things to do

12. How many each of ⌐⌐⌐⌐, ⌐⌐, ⌐ and ⌐. ⌐ are there in the next song?

13. Clap the rhythm of the song after the first note. Say the rhythm words 'walk', 'running', 'scampering' 'long jumping', 'hurdling' and 'supersonic'.
14. All practise the rhythms of (a) by repeating the rhythm words of each a given number of times. Now, in three groups, combine the first column, changing to the next rhythms of each

row at every signal. Repeat, clapping or playing contrasted percussion instruments or objects.

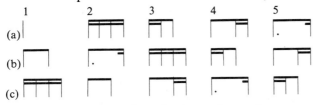

15. Echo these two-bar rhythms clapped to you. Echoes and rhythms are to follow continuously:

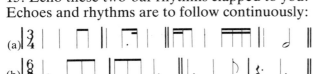

16. First clap each of the following, saying the rhythm words:

Later, divide into two groups and perform them simultaneously, or in succession as a canon with various delays. Finally, use contrasted un-pitched percussion.

17. Treat each pair of rhythms of 5 in the same time as in 16.

A song from Ireland: 'As I was Going Along the Road'

22

Things to do

18. Repeat previous activities, clapping or playing without the help of rhythm words.

19. Now sing the song with two pupils playing the rhythms of 16 starting at X. Use suitable contrasted unpitched percussion or musical objects. Repeat under a conductor.

20. Invent other rhythm word systems for

Keep each set in some category such as food, drink or towns. Remember, these can never be exact systems as the words can often be said in different ways. You will probably

have trouble with  Repeat some of the above activities using new word systems.

21. Repeat the rhythm dictation of 18 in Chapter 1. This time the gaps will be filled with

22. Now write down two- or four-bar $\frac{2}{4}$ rhythms played to you. You will be told which of the following will be included:

Interval of an octave

Things to do

23. Find how many 3rd and 5th jumps there are in 'As I was Going Along the Road'. There is just one other kind of jump. What interval is it?

The other interval is found at the beginning. You might have had trouble singing across the large gap of an 8th, or:

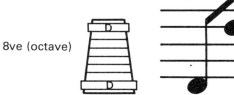

8ve (octave)

Compared with 3rds (line–line or space–space) and 5ths (line–line–line or space–space–space), octaves are less instantly recognised. However, it is often safe to guess that a big jump is an 8ve.

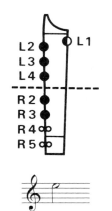

L2 L1
L3
L4
- - - - - -
R2
R3
R4
R5

○ Pinched hole

The next recorder note, and all those higher, require you to make a slight leak at the thumb hole. Bend your left thumb so that a narrow slit appears between the nail and the side of the hole. This action is called pinching.

Practise playing the 8ve between lower E and this upper E: . The fingering for lower and upper 8ves is usually the same—or very nearly so. Keep the left thumb in contact with the instrument, just rolling it in the hole. All higher notes need a firmer tonguing of 'too' and increased breath pressure.

Next, practise changing between upper D and E. Always land the thumb unpinched, immediately then rolling into the pinched position.

Now play the scale from middle C to upper E and back again, preferably in one breath. You are now able to play the last song.

Things to do

24. Hear interval jumps played up and down. Write 'yes' for 8ves and 'no' for other intervals. Now practise singing an 8ve above or below given pitches.

25. Each take or share a glockenspiel. Find a given starting note and move a beater silently up or down a selection of 3rds, 5ths and 8ves as directed. At a signal, all play. Recognise

'odd men out'. Score + or − points each time.

26. Identify intervals played up or down as 3rds, 5ths or 8ves. Repeat 25, this time 'shadowing' the same intervals as they are played from a given starting note.

27. As many as possible practise the parts given with the previous song.

28. Sing the song and/or play it on pitched percussion/recorder. Add the accompaniments of 19 and 27.

5 LATE BAROQUE

The Baroque period, which began with the first operas at the beginning of the seventeenth century, continued into the first half of the eighteenth century. Although many composers helped to develop opera and oratorio, other types of music became increasingly important.

A PASSION told the story of Christ's crucifixion and a CANTATA also usually used words from the Bible. Both these and oratorios had the story part set as recitative, accompanied by a bass instrument and keyboard continuo—just like opera.

In the solo SONATA and TRIO SONATA, one or two melody instruments were accompanied by the continuo players.

The orchestra, now based on the string family, was not only used in overtures and accompaniment. Composers also began to write orchestral pieces to be played on their own.

The Baroque CONCERTO usually contrasted the solo or trio sonata group (CONCERTINO) with the full string orchestra (RIPIENO or TUTTI).

The opening of a Handel concerto

The SUITE consisted of an overture or PRELUDE followed by a series of dances. These dances often included the slow triple-time SARABANDE, the quadruple-time GAVOTTE and BOURRÉE, the triple-time MINUET and the dotted beat GIGUE (JIG). Suites were written both for orchestra and solo instruments.

It was not only the suite that had different pieces in it. The other instrumental works such as the sonata and concerto also consisted of

different pieces called MOVEMENTS—so called because each one had a different tempo or 'movement' speed. From now onwards we shall be able to talk about 'first movements', 'slow movements' and so on.

Composers at this time were rarely independent or self-employed. They were treated more or less as servants by their royal or other masters, and their instrumental music was usually

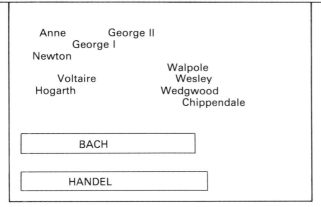

Anne   George II
     George I
Newton
                    Walpole
     Voltaire   Wesley
  Hogarth   Wedgwood
                    Chippendale

BACH

HANDEL

only heard by a select audience in private performances. Although the first public concerts had been started in England in the seventeenth century, ordinary folk still did not generally go to concerts as we do today.

At the end of the Baroque period many It-alian composers were still in the 'first division'. Arcangelo Corelli wrote concertos and sonatas, Antonio Vivaldi is particularly famous for his

Antonio Vivaldi

concertos featuring many different solo instruments and Domenico Scarlatti (actually working in Spain) wrote harpischord pieces. However, other countries were now coming on the scene. In France, Jean Philippe Rameau was noted for his operas, and both he and François Couperin were important composers of harpsichord suites. But the two giants of late Baroque music were both Germans. Johann Sebastian Bach and George Frederick Handel put their country at the top of the 'first division' for the first time—and there Germany stayed for the next two hundred years or so!

Johann Sebastian Bach

J. S. Bach was the greatest of a long line of family musicians. He was born in Eisenach (now in East Germany) in 1685. Bach was organist in several establishments before settling down as the overworked cantor (choir master) of St Thomas's Church in Leipzig. Here he taught in the adjacent school and wrote an enormous amount of music, including a cantata for his choir to sing each Sunday and organ music to play in the services. He also had many other duties to perform for the unappreciative church authorities.

Bach composed all types of music except opera. His best-known works include the *St Matthew Passion*, the *Brandenburg Concertos*, orchestral suites and many famous organ and

25

other keyboard works. He was married twice and had twenty children! Pianists may have played some of the pieces Bach wrote for his second wife Anna Magdalena. Not all his children survived, but several also became important composers.

Bach died in Leipzig in 1750. Perhaps you know of families with a history of talent in something like sport, art or music?

George Frederick Handel

Handel was also born in 1685, in Halle, but he never met Bach. His father wanted him to become a lawyer. He did not marry, and lived a more worldly life than the devout Bach, travelling widely before settling down as a naturalised Englishman in London.

Handel wrote many operas, concertos and orchestral suites, including the *Water Music* and *Fireworks Music*, but he is best known for his oratorio *Messiah*. It was this work and other oratorios that helped him dominate the musical life of England. By a strange coincidence, both Handel and Bach went blind in later life. He died in 1759 and was buried with great ceremony in Westminster Abbey.

This Evening the Remains of Mr. Handel will be buried in Weftminfter · Abbey. The Gentlemen of his Majefty's Chapels Royal, as well as the Choirs of St. Paul's and St. Peter's, will attend the Solemnity, and fing Dr. Croft's Funeral Anthem

From the *Public Advertiser*, 20 April 1759

The late Baroque style

Late Baroque music is usually easily recognised. One important 'fingerprint' is the continuo—the continuous bass part played by one keyboard and bass instruments. Here are some other clues:

Continuous regular rhythms that keep going like a machine.

Sequences where you can often guess what is going to happen next.

Imitation between the parts. When there is any kind of musical 'conversation' between instruments or voices it is called COUNTERPOINT. CONTRAPUNTAL music gives everybody a share of the tunes.

Unchanging instrumentation. Either one group or volume level throughout or sudden contrasts between just two groups or volume levels.

(a) Listen to different late Baroque pieces. Discuss which of the above 'fingerprints' appear in each.
(b) Recognise dance movements as sarabande, minuet, gavotte or gigue.

In your notebook

(i) Explain the following in your own words: Passion, Suite, Movement and Counterpoint.
(ii) Write a few sentences comparing the lives and music of Bach and Handel.

Assignments

(A) Collect material associated with the life and music of this time.
(B) List English people who could have met Handel in London.
(C) Trace or draw a sketch map of Europe. Show the position of London, Halle, Eisenach, and Leipzig. Indicate their connection with Bach or Handel.

6 CAN'T STOP— NO BRAKES

The four-bar phrase

Have you ever watched waves breaking regularly on the beach? Nothing can stop them. The closer they get to their breaking point the more certain this seems.

The notes in each bar of music also behave rather like a wave. Their breaking point is the first beat of the next bar. The closer notes get to it, the harder it is to stop them—especially when they are 'supersonic':

'I was go-ing a - long'

Bar lines are not built to stop anything. Their purpose is to show where each wave of notes breaks. The first beat accents are like magnets, drawing the previous notes to them. Oddly, beat *ones* are usually endings, not beginnings!

Things to do

1. These are from two previous song openings:

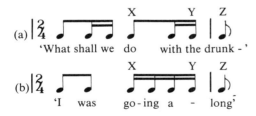

(a) 'What shall we do with the drunk -'

(b) 'I was go-ing a - long'

Sing each (or clap its rhythm), stopping in turn at X, Y and Z. Where was it hardest to stop?

Finally, discuss why it is often bad for musicians to practise just one bar at a time.

2. Now similarly clap this rhythm, stopping at the letters in alphabetical order:

'Jin-gle bells, jin-gle bells, Jin-gle all the way.'

In 1, the hardest place to 'put on the brakes' was at the end of the bar, especially when the tempo was fast. Did anyone skid at Y?

It was much easier to stop at Z, where the first 'wave' of notes broke:

But in 2, the first beats were not equally easy to stop at. Most people unconsciously add them up, and feel that the fourth accent (W) or possibly the second (Z) is where the music is leading to.

The normal musical phrase is therefore two or four bars long.

Things to do

3. Clap or sing each of the following openings, at first omitting the last word:
(a) 'John Brown's body lies a moulding in the grave.'
(b) 'Land of hope and glory.'
(c) 'Ten green bottles hanging on the wall.'
(d) 'I've got a lovely bunch of coconuts.'
Now repeat, finishing at the last word.

Even at the end, did you not feel a little off-balance—and want to continue?

4. Now clap or sing the songs of 3 to the end.

(a) Hear dances from Bach or Handel suites. After beating time, identify the dances from those given on page 24. Count the phrases.

Musical sentences

A single line of poetry, like a question without an answer, cannot satisfy us. Similarly, a single musical phrase needs to be followed by at least one more. Most music consists of many phrases. The phrasing of sung music matches the phrases or lines of the words. Music for instruments is also usually phrased just as regularly. Each two or four-bar 'questioning' phrase is balanced by an 'answering' one of similar length.

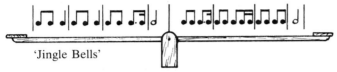

'Jingle Bells'

The shortest complete musical SENTENCE or tune is one of just two phrases. Really long pieces are like conversations or stories, with many phrases, sentences and paragraphs. The main difference between them is that musical phrases, like those of most poems, are much more regular. Imagine a story with the same number of words in each phrase or sentence!

It is helpful to think of musical commas, full stops and other punctuation coming between the phrases. At these points there is often a longer note. Even if it is a whole bar long the musical heart beat rarely comes to a halt—even at 'full stops'.

It sometimes helps a performer to play musically or breathe in the right place if the phrasing is marked in some way. This is done by using a long slur. Do not confuse the various uses and names given to the slur. Three of them could have been used in the song on page 22.

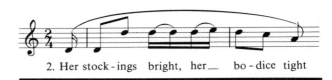

2. Her stock-ings bright, her— bo-dice tight

In your notebook

(i) Copy the above song opening on a treble stave. Label phrasing slur, syllable slur and tie.
(ii) (Copy, unjumbling the words)
Musical *pashers* are sometimes two, but usually four bars long. The shortest piece is a musical *nee scent* of just *owt* phrases. Phrases and sentences often end with *glon* notes.

Things to do

5. Pretend that four-bar rhythms clapped to you are 'questions'. All reply by clapping a rhythm that seems to 'answer' it nicely. It could be the same one again, but try to be different. Just let yourself go, starting when you feel you should. Did anything unusual occur at the beginning and end of your 'answers'?
6. Without looking at the music, clap 'answers' to the question rhythms at the foot of the page. Discuss why your 'answers' (i) started immediately with (a) were delayed with (b) and (ii) ended together.
7. In two or more groups, clap/say the words of 3 in succession as a canon with a one-line delay. Later, experiment with (i) shorter delays down to one beat, (ii) silent performances in your head, but with a final loud 'nuts'. (How will the 'nuts' show if you have kept in time?)
8. Repeat 5–7 after reading the following. Feel the appropriate phrase—join beats.

Your answers should all have ended together because of your unconscious counting up to the fourth accent. They also began together because you matched the beginning of each 'question' and 'answer'. In 6, for example, your 'internal clock' continued counting beats so that both 'answers' began on beat one. There was no need to wait in (a). However, in (b) you had to wait for a long bar to finish. The waiting seems part of the 'question':

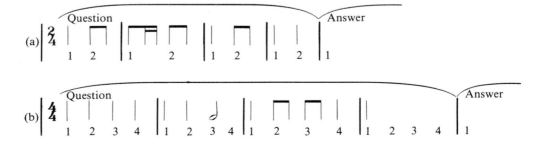

The following harpsichord piece was written by Bach for his second wife. The RH and LH staves of keyboard music are always bracketed together. The RH includes many sequential two- and one-bar patterns. Provided the rhythm is the same, sequences need not involve the exact repetition of every interval. Although Bach did not approve of the recently invented piano, this minuet is now usually played on that instrument:

From the notebook for Anna Magdalena: **Minuet**   **J. S. Bach**

(b) Clap the RH rhythm and then follow the music as the above piece is played on the piano or in a recording. During further playings:

(i) Beat time with the music;
(ii) Clap with the RH part;
(iii) Compare the editor's dynamics with those performed. Are they possible on a harpsichord?
(iv) Indicate the bar and beat number where the music is suddenly stopped.

This minuet is a musical paragraph of two sentences. The given slurs indicate two and four-bar phrases. Identify (v) where the first sentence ends, (vi) where the remaining phrasing slurs should be put, (vii) each sequence, pointing out where the repetition is inexact.

Finally find out if any instrumental players have had to practise this or other pieces by Bach.

Things to do

9. In the RH part, find (a) the letter names of the highest and lowest notes, (b) the number of crotchet Gs.

10. Clap the rhythm of the given RH part while just the LH is played, counting the beats. Now write the LH rhythm of the missing bars, first hearing each bar on its own if necessary.

11. Practise the parts given with the minuet. As many as possible accompany it played on the piano (or a recording if you are in tune with it). Finally, add the rhythms of Chapter 4 (5(a) and 15(a)) as repeated ostinati on unpitched percussion.

12. Turn Bach's minuet into a pop song. It first needs to be changed into quadruple time. This is how the RH will begin:

Listen to it played in this variation while following the normal music. Have a competition to see who can write the best words. Sing the winning entry and then add an accompaniment. Either improvise one or use the rhythms of 11 modified by adding a crotchet or crotchet rest at the beginning of each bar.

Choose from these instruments: side drum and rhythm brushes, tambourine, triangle, wood block, sandpaper block, maracas and jingle stick. Use any home-made examples.

Later, add the parts given with the minuet

modified as above (with rest or repeated first note).

13. First compose a rhythmic sentence of two four-bar phrases in $\frac{2}{4}$ or $\frac{3}{4}$ time. Make the last note of each phrase fill a complete bar.

Now turn this rhythm into a melody. Use these notes of the pentatonic scale from G:

Begin and end on the home note G and end the first phrase on a different note. Avoid any jumps bigger than a 3rd. Why will you need to plan your tune first?

Listen to them all played on the piano. Vote for the best and give yourself five extra votes if you recognise your tune. Now, with the winning tunes written on the board:

(a) All play/sing (solfa) each one;
(b) Combine different tunes in the same time, or sing one in canon.

14. Here is a quiz. Write or discuss the answers.

(a) Why does a bell stop ringing when you hold it?
(b) What are the differences between beat, time and rhythm?
(c) How many centuries ago were Bach and Handel born?
(d) How many octaves can the average person sing?
(e) When can a crotchet be longer than a minim?

(c) Bach's music is popular with modern arrangers. Listen to the previous Minuet or other dance movements sung, 'swung' or otherwise modernised.

If appropriate, add improvised rhythmic percussion to the recording, as above.

Assignments

(A) After relegation from the musical 'first division' in the seventeenth century, Britain had a low musical reputation until recently. This has extended to other things as well. Find examples of any use of foreign names—just to make things sound impressive or of high quality.

(B) Write an imaginary letter from Handel in London to Bach in Leipzig, describing how busy you are. Then write Bach's reply.

The violin family

At the end of the Baroque period the popularity of the orchestra and more public concerts meant that the gentler lute and viola had to give way to the louder violin family. This particular family of stringed instruments has been the foundation of the orchestra ever since. Each member of it has four strings and shares the same basic shape:

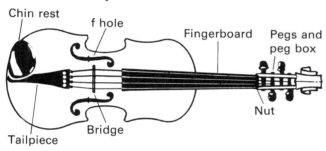

They are usually played by stroking the strings with a bow:

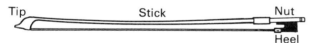

But they can also be played PIZZ(ICATO) by plucking the strings with a finger. In this case, a return to bowing is indicated by ARCO.

Two strings played simultaneously is called DOUBLE STOPPING:

In the Baroque period the bows were more rounded than they are today. This means that triple and even quadruple stopping were then easier to do properly:

Each string is tuned by turning a peg to tighten or slacken it. Sometimes screw adjusters on the strings make the job easier. The open strings of each instrument are tuned to these pitches:

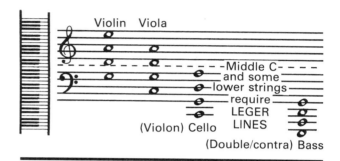

Things to do

1. Look at the above staves and notes. Discuss (a) the interval made between the open strings of each instrument, (b) why strings of the same length can have a different pitch, (c) why pushing the treble and bass staves together makes some of the intervals clearer, (d) why these staves are normally pushed apart.

2. Watch any string players tune their open strings. If they tune to the piano, discuss whether strings are sharp or flat. Now listen to (a) all four open strings of each instrument played in succession, using separate bow strokes/a single bow stroke, (b) adjacent strings bowed together (double stopping). What interval mixture does each make? (c) different notes made by stopping just one string.

Discuss (i) what makes double stopping difficult, (ii) why triple and quadruple stopping is not strictly possible.

Now watch a demonstration of pizzicato and the rapid bowing of one string (tremolo). Finally, any pupil players can play prepared pieces.

(a) Hear recordings demonstrating the different members of the violin family played solo. Recognise pizzicato, tremolo and double stopping. (b) Identify the violin, viola, cello and double bass as each is featured as a solo or group.

The score

Overleaf is a piece for string orchestra by Bach. Like all orchestral music, you will expect to hear at least several players in each string part. In string music slurs indicate notes to be played with a single bow stroke. The violins, divided into 'firsts' and 'seconds' (Vl. I, II), also have their staves bracketed together. The continuo part is a feature of most Baroque music. There may not be a harpsichord in modern performances.

When each part is written like this on a separate stave, the music is called an OPEN (FULL or ORCHESTRAL) SCORE. A double bar (line) is used at the end of main sections. A ⌢ indicates a PAUSE on that note/rest.

(c) Listen to this Air played by a string orchestra. Discuss:
(i) Whether a continuo harpsichord is also used;
(ii) Whether the repeats are varied by using fewer instruments or ornamentation;
(iii) Which other Baroque 'fingerprints' the music features (see page 26);
(iv) Why an Air is an unusual movement for a suite;
(v) Why there is no conductor in the above picture.

Now listen again, following the first violin part with a finger or your eye. At a signal, indicate where the music has got to. Follow the same part again, this time listening to the second violins while the firsts hold long notes in bars 3, 4 and later. Listen particularly at X, where the parts are next door. 2nds can sound nice!

With the bass control turned up, follow the 'walking' bass continuo part up to the first time bar. Listen very carefully at the end and in bar 1. Why is the bass particularly important in these bars? Now (vi) listen with the bass control turned down, (vii) hear bars 1 and 2 of the first violin part alone on the piano. The distortion (by 8ves) of what is basically a descending scale is typically 'Baroque'.

In the Baroque period the bass was as important as the part(s) playing the tune(s). Without it, especially during long notes, the Baroque 'machine' stops and the music seems to die.

For a change, listen to the Air in modern arrangements. Discuss which you prefer.

In your notebook

(iv)(Copy, unjumbling the letters)
The *nope* strings of the violin, viola and cello are an interval of a fifth apart. The double bass's strings are a *hot fur* apart. The notes of the violin are written on the *belter* stave. The *locel* and double bass both use the bass stave.

The viola's notes require a special *vaste* and the C clef.

Notes above or below any stave have to be put on *gleer* lines.

Orchestral music when written on separate staves is in open *cores*.

Interval of a 4th

Things to do

9. Find the letter names of the highest and lowest notes in each part of the Air.
10. Write the last bar of the viola part (a) on a treble stave, (b) on a bass stave. Remember, the note stems may have to change direction. It is clear why the alto clef is also called a C clef. Suggest why the usual clefs can also be called the G and F clefs.
11. Count the number of (a) 3rd, (b) 5th, (c) 8ve jumps in the second violin part. Discuss how each is recognised.
12. Each take a pitched class instrument. From a given starting letter move your finger up or down a 3rd, 5th or 8ve as directed. After a number of moves check your position. Score + and − points.
13. From any given starting pitch, identify the next note as being (a) a 2nd or 3rd above or below, (b) a 3rd or 5th above or below, (c) a 5th or 8ve above or below. It may help to step across each interval in your head, counting the starting note as 'one'.
14. Repeat 12 but this time following 2nds, 3rds, 5ths or 8ves by sound as they are played.

15. Now revise the sound of these same intervals played together as mixtures on the piano:

8ve   'like one note'
2nd   'clashing'
3rds 'pleasant', 'normal'
5th   'bare', 'oriental', 'medieval' (and string tuning)

Identify (a) single examples, (b) rows of each interval. Which is easier to do?

Do you remember why the interval of a 4th will have much the same flavour as a 5th? Just tip any 5th upside down either way. Inverting the same letters will not affect the sound much:

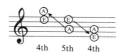

This also explains why the violin's open string 5ths ascending are the same letters as the double bass's 4ths descending:

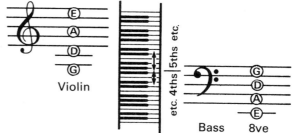

4ths are not quite as quickly recognised on the stave as 3rds and 5ths. Like 2nds and 8ves, they can never neatly occupy two spaces or two lines. Remember, whenever possible play instruments by jumping intervals—not by reading letters. Here is a reminder of all the intervals learnt so far:

Tunes like the following that do not begin on beat one often start with an upward 4th (s,–d). This famous song was written by a British composer while Handel was living in London. It was part of an aristocratic entertainment called a MASQUE. These consisted of music, dancing, acting, processions and pageantry.

(d) Follow the music through a performance of 'Rule Britannia'. There may be other verses. Discuss:
  (i) Why there are slurs against groups of notes;
  (ii) Why the music for 'Arose' and 'never' is good word painting;
(iii) The meaning of the dots above the quavers near the beginning of the chorus.

'Rule, Britannia!'   Dr Arne

Staccato and legato

A dot over or under a note tells the performer to sing or play in a detached way or STACCATO (pronounced 'Stir carto'). Staccato notes: ♩ ♩ ♩ are therefore performed shorter than they are written:

■ ■ ■   But their separation by unwritten rests means that they are not faster. The xylophone and plucked strings (pizzicato) always have a staccato effect. The opposite of staccato is LEGATO (pronounced 'lee garto'). This is the normal, smooth and connected style of performance.

Things to do

16. Assemble violin-type instruments available for class use (dangling LH fingers could substitute for 'strings').

First stand each instrument upright on the floor or a table, holding all types rather like a sideways cello:

Anchor the thumb and always play by feel, looking at the music. Pluck each open string (finger) in order, as you look at it on its particular stave. This will remind you that next-door strings are not next-door notes. Next, look at the part for your instrument. Discuss:
(a) Why there is only one alternative viola note:
(b) Why the cello notes usually appear to be lower than those of the double bass.
Finally, practise finding the notes of your part. You will not have to jump across any strings. Do not play in rhythm yet.
17. Practise the given parts and then accompany the singing of the chorus. The open string jumping 5ths could also be played on class instruments at any 8ve. They will require very slow practising at first. Think of each jump as twice times next-door-but-one. This chorus is often used for football match chanting. Make up your own chants to sing.
18. Count the number of 4th jumps in the above song. What is the biggest interval used?
19. Repeat 12–15, replacing 5ths with 4ths.
20. Repeat the melody dictation of 33 of Chapter 2. This time the notes used will be chosen from either 30(a) or (b). You will have to recognise jumps of a 3rd, 4th and 5th.

Assignment

(A) Illustrate your notebook with further material on stringed instruments. Include pictures and information on present-day players as well. (The *Radio Times* or record magazines can help you.)

8 MAJOR ROAD AHEAD

The dotted one-beat note

Things to do

1. In two groups, repeatedly clap the rhythm of the chorus opening 'Rule, Britannia' against its beat. Without looking at the music, work out the note value of the first note.

The first note lasts for one-and-a-half beats. There are two ways of writing it:
(a) Using a tie to join a

♩ to a ♪ :
(b) Using a dot to make

a ♩ half as long again: 'Sausages on sticks' show how the dotted part pushes into the next beat:
A one-and-a-half beat note can be counted: e.g. or rhythm words can be used. For example:

'Rule___ Bri tannia'

1 (2) & 3 &

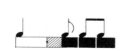

'walk (run)-ning, 'run-ning'

Notes longer than a beat are best counted.

Do not confuse ♩. when a one-and-a-half beat note: $\frac{2}{4}$ ♩.   ♪
1   2 &

with ♩. when a one-beat note: $\frac{6}{8}$ ♩. ♫♫
1   2

(or with ♩ —a staccato crotchet!)

When ♩. is a one-and-a-half beat note, you must not hurry the beat on the dot. You will also be tempted to play the next note on this beat.

Things to do

2. Practise clapping these following ostinati:

(a) $\frac{3}{4}$ ♩. ♪   (b) $\frac{3}{4}$ ♩ ♩. ♪   (c) $\frac{3}{4}$ ♩. ♪
1(2) & 3   1 2 (3)&   1(2) & 3 &

(d) $\frac{4}{4}$ ♩. ♪♩   (e) $\frac{4}{4}$ ♩ ♩. ♪
1(2) & 3 4   1 2(3) & 4

3. In groups, combine (a)–(c), clapping or using contrasted percussion. Similarly combine (d)–(e).
4. (a) Recognise which of the above ostinati is played to you.
(b) Write down the rhythm of other ostinati played to you using the above values.
(c) Write down the rhythm of two- or four-bar phrases played to you. You will be told the time and which of the above values are to be used.
5. Clap the rhythm of the following song as far as the chorus, before hearing it. The counting is started for you. Now follow the music as it is played. In what ways are its first two notes similar to the opening of the song on page 36? Practise the solfa 'track', including the s₁–t₁ 3rd and s₁–d 4th, before singing any part to solfa.
6. The tambourine and wood block parts combine ♩ and ♩. beats. Practise clapping and saying the ostinati separately (at the same beat tempo) before adding to your performance.

A cowboy song: 'Old Paint'

Sharps and flats

3 & 1(2)& 3 & 1 2 3 & 1 2 3 12

Things to do

7. Revise 'The major scale' in Chapter 2.
8. Here is the opening phrase of 'The First Nowell' in key C. There are no jumps:
(a) Clap its rhythm while counting the beats,
(b) Play on any instruments, (c) sing to solfa.

9. Sing the above in keys F and G after hearing each track played. What letters must you start from? It may go too high for your voices.
10. Try to play 'The First Nowell' on a diatonic (C) class instrument in keys F (start on A) and G (start on B) as well as C. Discuss what goes wrong. Now play 'white' note scales from F and G.

There are no problems with key C major:

The white notes make the major scale interval pattern:

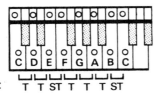

But when you start from G the pattern goes wrong at F

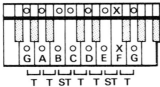

The E–F interval is too small. It needs to be a tone

So, the F is raised (sharpened) a semitone in key G major:

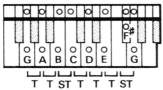

F SHARP (F♯) replaces F NATURAL (F♮) to make the pattern correct

When you start from F the pattern goes wrong at B

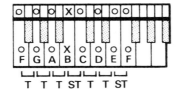

The A–B interval is too large. It needs to be a semitone

So, the B is lowered (flattened) a semitone in key F major

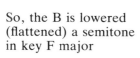 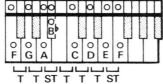

B FLAT (B♭) replaces B NATURAL (B♮) to make the pattern correct

Remember, a ♯ just raises a note by a semitone. It has got nothing to do with a sharp sound—or taste or point! Similarly, a flat just lowers a note by a semitone.

Further, the fact that black keys are *raised* above white ones has nothing to do with the effect of a ♯. After all, black keys can also be flats!

Key signatures

Performers need to be told when any letter is to be sharpened or flattened. Any sharp(s) or flat(s) required are put at the beginning, before the time signature. This is the music's KEY SIGNATURE. It appears at the beginning of every line as a constant reminder!

Here are the key signatures of G major

and F major

Each ♯ or ♭ is written on just one particular line or space. However, it affects every 8ve of that letter. Key C major does not require a signature (open key).

Things to do

11. Take the front off an upright piano. Look at the different hammer patterns as a suitable flat object presses down an 8ve of white keys from C–C, G–G and F–F. Compare each pattern with the above diagram for that starting point. Now watch the hammers as each of these three 'all-white' scales is slowly played. Listen for any places where the familiar major scale sound is modified. Repeat, but this time follow the O and X on the appropriate diagram. At the same time, say tone or semitone as indicated for each step. Be prepared for what happens at each X. Discuss whether notes can be heard/seen as 'black' or 'white' on non-keyboard instruments.

12. Repeat 10. This time use a chromatic instrument, playing F# or B♭ when necessary.

13. Now play the chorus of 'Rule, Britannia' on a chromatic instrument. At first ignore the F# and hear the tune go wrong when you play F ♮. Now play it correctly in G major, using the F#.

14. Turn to page 13 and sing 'Turn the Glasses Over' again. Now draw a glockenspiel diagram, showing the notes required to play this song. Next, use either diatonic or chromatic instruments to play it. The tune is in key F. Why is no B♭ required?

15. Write the solfa track of notes required for this song. Find the solfa names of the notes making each interval of a 4th. Now sing this solfa track, followed by the song itself also to solfa.

In your notebook

(i) (Copy, completing the words)
All major scales except C require one or more sh____ or fl____ to make the correct tone and s____ pattern.

The k____ s____, put at the beginning of every line, shows which letters need changing. A sh____ raises every o____ of that letter a s____, while a fl____ lowers notes a s____. The t____ s____ is always written after the key signature.

(ii) Draw and label the key signatures of G and F major on both treble and bass staves.

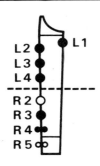

Recorder players must now learn the 'black' notes required for playing in keys G and F—but there is nothing black about them on the recorder! They both have forked fingering.

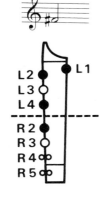

Repeat Activity 13, using the recorder. Now play this chorus a tone lower in key F by 'ear'. Finally, play the first two bars of 'The First Nowell' in keys C, F and G, also by 'ear'. Remember the following whenever you play:
(a) Hold the instrument correctly.
(b) Cover the holes snugly.
(c) Listen to your own playing—but do not try to drown the others!
(d) Aim to be perfectly in tune. If you are flat, slightly increase the air pressure (and vice versa).
(e) Breathe only between phrases. Make your air last by squeezing it out gently.
(f) In legato playing apply a continuous, gentle air pressure (like 'squirting' a balloon). Also, do not think of stopping a note as a separate action before starting the next one. Think only of starting notes—the stopping then happens automatically.

Here is the previous song TRANSPOSED from key F major to key G major:

A new key for: 'Old Paint'

Things to do

16. First perform the song with as many of the accompaniments as possible. Add the ostinato unpitched percussion parts from its key F version on page 38. Now play the tune incorrectly with an F♮ . Next, try playing it in key F while looking at the key G music. It will mean starting one letter lower and then jumping the same intervals as before. If you find this difficult, play from the music on page 38. Can you explain (a) why no B^b is needed in this key F version? (b) Why musical signatures, unlike those on letters, always come at the beginning?

17. Turn to page 38. Write the accompanying melodic part for 'Old Paint' on manuscript paper, one letter higher in key G. Also use the proper key and time signatures. Play the transposed tune on class instruments/recorder. Later, add this part to the key G version accompaniment.

18. Now write the chorus of 'Rule Britannia' (page 36) in key F. Play on instruments as in 17.

Music for the Royal Fireworks

The following Minuet is from the suite of dances known as the *Fireworks Music*. Handel wrote them for a celebration ordered by King George II to mark the end of the War of Austrian Succession. The titles for some of the movements suggest that a form of word-painting was intended. When Handel added string parts to the original woodwind and brass SCORING (ORCHESTRATION), the military complained to the Comptroller of His Majesty's Fireworks:

> 'Now Hendel proposes to lessen the number of trumpets, etc. and to have violeens. I dont at all doubt but when the King hears it he will be very much displeased.'

The first performance in London's Green Park in 1749 was combined with a fireworks display. The music was a success but the fireworks were an anti-climax. One of the set-piece structures caught fire—and it rained!

It was the custom for the different movements of a suite to be in the same key—in this case D major. It is rather like the way we expect the different parts of a suit or the pieces of furniture in a dining room or bedroom suite to have the same colour or style. This minuet has been transposed into key G and SCORED for class instruments.

If you sing the minuet's melody (or any other music) to solfa, first practise the given 'track' and then any indicated intervals. Open-string players will also have to practise crossing strings by feel before their part can be played.

Things to do

19. Clap the minuet's rhythm before hearing it. Use the counting method.

20. Improvise a tune on a class instrument (two beaters) in the rhythm of this Minuet. Use only the notes of the G pentatonic scale as given in Chapter 6, 13.

21. Take turns playing the same notes (in any order) in the rhythms of well-known songs. See who can identify the song first.

22. This Minuet begins with notes d–s. It is far more common to begin s–d (like the last song). Make a list of songs/pieces beginning this way.

23. Find the old spellings in the previous column. Violinists often refer to their instrument by a nickname. (a) What is it? (b) Why is it so called?

24. When you have performed the Minuet in various ways, play the tune in key F on class instrument/recorder. There are three ways of doing this:
(a) Start on F and play by ear, without music;
(b) As (a) but let the intervals up and down help you;
(c) First write it out in key F.
Discuss which method(s) best suit each instrument.

The fireworks display in London's Green Park

Arranged from the *Fireworks Music*: Minuet I

Handel

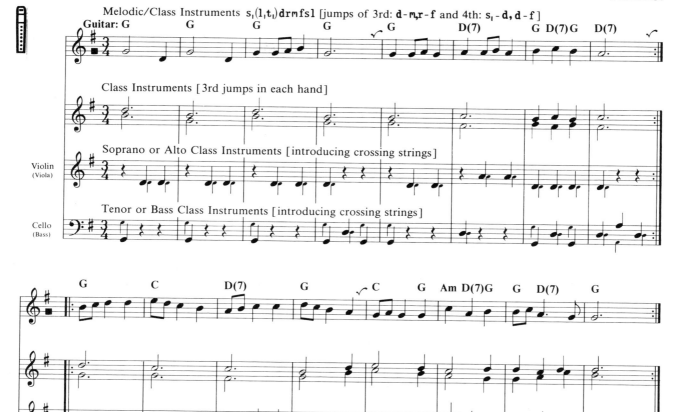

(a) Listen to a recording of Handel's *Fireworks Music*. Nowadays it is played in several different arrangements. Compare different versions if you can:

Overture
After a solemn opening comes 'La Guerra' (War). What groups of instruments play 'question and answer' phrases at the beginning of 'War'? Discuss how Handel suggests war.

Bourrée
A dance similar to a gavotte. Work out its time. What instrument plays the perky Baroque bass part?

Siciliana
A slow dance with a quadruple ♩. beat, representing 'La Paix' (Peace). Beat time very slowly as it is played. Are any instruments omitted from this? Why is this a good idea?

'La Rejouissance' (Rejoicing)
Why is this piece good word-painting?

Minuets I and II
Each minuet is in two sections (Ia, b and IIa, b). Both the sections and the minuets may be repeated. Follow the above music through all the repetitions and then write the symbols of what was played in your performance(s) (e.g.: Ia, Ia, Ib, etc.). Where is the two-bar sequence in Minuet I?

Listen to the bourrée and minuets again. Notice if any ornamentation (shakes, etc.) is used and whether repeats are played differently or with different instruments.

Finally, discuss:
(i) Which you prefer of any different performances regarding tempi, instruments used and ornamentation;
(ii) Which movements you like/dislike;
(iii) Why the military complained about Handel's revised scoring.

9 LOOK, NO HANDS!

Anacrusis

Things to do

1. Repeat Chapter 6 (5–8).
2. The following 'question' phrases do not begin on a strong beat:

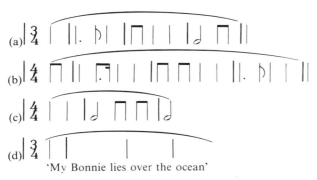

(a) | (b) | (c) | (d)

'My Bonnie lies over the ocean'

All clap an answering phrase as each is clapped to you. Even if you know (d), you need not answer according to the song. Discuss:
(i) How the beginning of each question and answer matched each other;
(ii) Why the answer to (d) was particularly delayed.

When a 'question' rhythm begins on a weak beat, you feel the beginning of your 'answer' should match it. For example, as 2(a) begins on

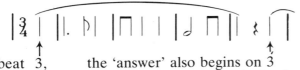

beat 3,   the 'answer' also begins on 3

One or more weak beat note(s) at the beginning of any phrase (an ANACRUSIS) do not normally make it any longer. Their value is subtracted from its last bar. This enables the next phrase to begin in the same way. The final bar of music will also be similarly shortened.

What works with bars of music also works with bars of chocolate—and even with elephants behind bars!

Or you could imagine this happening:

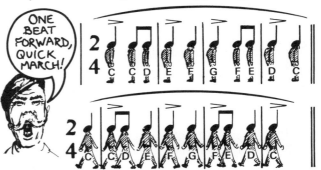

However, although marching forward does not affect the length of a phrase (or the way bars are numbered):

you will discover that the change of accents makes a big difference to its musical effect. The beat numbers show how a conductor can start both kinds of music. The whole or part of an introductory bar (or the remainder of the anacrusis bar) is counted or beaten.

Things to do

3(a) Clap the above two rhythms. Although their note values are the same, their rhythmic effect is very different if you accent correctly.
(b) Play/sing them to solfa or 'la', again accenting correctly. Have you made the same notes sound like different tunes?

44

An anacrusis does not affect the general need to have an even number of strong beats in a phrase. Your answering phrase to rhythm 2(d) had to wait for the fourth strong beat of the 'question' to arrive:

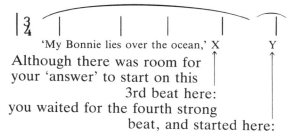

'My Bonnie lies over the ocean,' X   Y

Although there was room for
your 'answer' to start on this
          3rd beat here:
you waited for the fourth strong
          beat, and started here:

Things to do

4. Clap an 'answer' to 2(d), deliberately starting early at X. When you 'answer' more naturally at Y, did you nod the fourth strong beat?

5. Write out the rhythm of 2(d) without the words. Discuss the choice of note value(s), tie and rests possible at the end. Next, all clap an answering phrase as before. If you can, write this down as well.

6. Which of these songs begins (a) on a strong beat, (b) with a s_1–d anacrusis?

'What shall we do with the drunken sailor?', 'Turn the glasses over', 'Summer is icumen in', 'Rule, Britannia' (verse), 'Jim along Josie', 'Old Paint', 'My grandfather's clock', 'Haul away Joe', 'Water come a me eye', 'Lilli Burlero', 'Doh, ray, me', 'Salt, mustard, vinegar' and 'My old man's a dustman'. Now check that the (b) songs all have a shorter final bar.

Discuss what is unusual about the beginning of the last song's first two phrases.

7. If you have a song or hymn-book, find out whether strong beat or anacrusis starts are the more common. Discuss what this has to do with poetry. Look at a poetry book if you can.

Chorale preludes

Bach was very fond of using hymn tunes in his works. The tunes of the German Lutheran Church are called CHORALES (pronounced 'cor rarls'). The many pieces and movements he wrote that disguised or varied a chorale are known as CHORALE PRELUDES. His favourite method was to chop up the tune

into bits

and write another continuous tune to go with it.

The end of each phrase in chorales and hymn tunes is often shown by a ⌢ or double bar. The pause need not be obeyed.

The work overleaf includes two choral preludes. The complicated first one begins with an orchestral introduction. As the whole or parts of this reappear from time to time, it is called the RITORNELLO (Italian: 'return'). The repeating Purcell tune on page 11 could also be called a ritornello.

(a) Listen to movements from 'Sleepers, Wake!':
Final chorale
First get to know the chorale. Many Bach cantatas end simply like this. His church congregation would have known the hymn and could have sung with the choir. Why are the last two ‖ in the middle of a bar?
Fourth movement
Follow the string part given overleaf. See if you can guess when the singers are going to come in, this time with the chorale phrases varied. What section of the choir is used? When the recording is repeated (i) note the bar number of each chorale entry, (ii) compare each varied phrase with the chorale.

Now just study the music.
(iii) How many times does Bach use the opening phrase X–Y (including repeats)? (iv) In which bar does this phrase occur at a higher pitch in another key? (v) The music opens with the familiar rising 4th anacrusis. However, after this the frequent unexpected large jumps make it unusual. List the intervals greater than a 4th in X–Y. (vi) Compare the phrase at Z with its previous appearance.
(d) *First movement*
The opening orchestral ritornello begins with impressive 'engine' rhythms followed by scales.
(i) Count the number of times this jerky rhythm returns between the singing sections.
(ii) Follow the widely separated phrases of the chorale in long notes. Which section sings these while the rest of the choir has other music?
(iii) Which keyboard instrument plays the continuo part?
(b) Hear the fourth movement in (i) Bach's own organ arrangement, (ii) a modern version.

From Cantata 140:   'Sleepers, Wake!'   **Bach**

Fourth Movement Theme

The organ

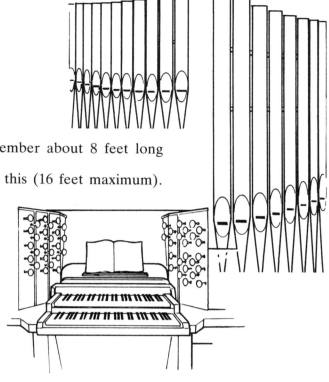

The simplest organ has a single row of pipes, one pipe for each key of the keyboard. Most organs, however, have many such rows of pipes, and more than one keyboard. In Bach's day large bellows supplying air to the pipes would have been pumped by hand. Nowadays, electric pumps are used.

The rows of pipes that have their longest member about 8 feet long sound the normal pitch expected for each key.

There are also rows of pipes twice as long as this (16 feet maximum). These sound notes an 8ve lower than expected.

Similarly, the rows half as long (4 feet maximum) produce notes an 8ve too high. There can be rows of pipes starting from 2 feet and even, occasionally, 32 feet.

Sets of pipes can sound very different from each other—just as wind instruments can be very different. Their sound depends on whether they are made of wood or metal, their diameter and many other things. Some even attempt to copy orchestral instruments. STOPS or TABS control which of the rows of pipes (RANKS) is available to the player.

Most stops or tabs have names explaining the sort of sound expected. As no two organs are alike, and as stops with the same name rarely make the same sounds, playing at an unfamiliar CONSOLE is quite an adventure.

Stops also have a number indicating the length in feet of the longest pipe in the rank. For example:

With the above stops out, an organist playing just middle C would sound:

There are also stops which give mixtures of different pitches. The average organ has two keyboards (MANUALS). These are called the

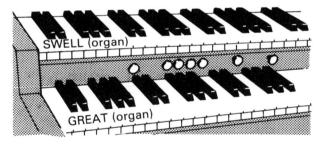

Each organ keyboard operates its own ranks of pipes. The pipes of the swell organ are boxed in. It gets its name from the Venetian blind in one side, operated by a foot pedal. This enables the volume to swell or diminish.

Most organs also have another secret keyboard. This is the PEDAL (organ) on the floor. As it is played by the feet the pedal board has extra large keys. The pedal part is written on a third (bass) stave.

As the feet usually play the bass part, the pedal organ always includes a 16-foot rank. Gadgets help players change things quickly (while playing!). For example,
foot or hand PISTONS operate groups of stops. COUPLERS cause the pipes of one keyboard to be played on another.

In your notebook

(i) (Copy, unjumbling the words)
The average *grona* has two *body rakes* arranged like steps, called the swell and the *gater*. There is also a *plade broad* played by the *teef*.

The *groanist* pulls out *spots* to change the sound quality.

Fugue

An organist can play with the RH on one keyboard, the LH on another and the feet on the pedalboard. This means that with suitable stops, three contrasting sounds can be played simultaneously on a two-manual instrument. Different sounds can also be quickly contrasted by jumping between keyboards. The organ is therefore very suitable for playing Baroque contrapuntal music. But how would you like to read three staves simultaneously, and play with both hands and both feet at the same time?

The organ is perfect for the many chorale preludes Bach wrote for it. The chorale on one keyboard can be made to have a very different sound from the accompanying parts played on other keyboards. The stops a player uses is called the REGISTRATION.

The organ is also very good for playing a FUGUE. A fugue is like a complicated round.

Extracts from: 'Jig' Fugue   **Bach**

Manuals (Subject)

A part introduces a S U B J E C T

5 A second part follows with the same S U B J E C T (or A N S W E R) at a different pitch

10 Both continue with general 'chat', often about the subject
etc.
to

Any other parts then take their turn to have the S U B J E C T etc.

25 Manuals

etc.

Pedal (Subject or 'Answer')

As it is a musical 'conversation', each part can be called a VOICE—whether sung or played on instruments. As the conversation continues, the subject reappears from time to time in each part. It gets quite kicked around.

Occasionally a voice is silent.

In German notation, B is H and B^b is B. This has enabled several composers to write fugues on the name BACH.

48

(c) Beat $\frac{12}{8}(\downarrow)$ time and count the bars as you follow the given music. Continue (i) noting the bar where the third voice enters with the subject (ii) ready to follow the pedal entry at bar 25. How many entries are there after bar 25?

Are there any further entries in the pedal?

Which part has the last word? Name the key. Listen again. Notice the sequences in the subject and elsewhere. Does the player (iii) jump between manuals, (iv) change registration? What makes it a 'jig'?

(d) Hear any organ work based on 'BACH'.

Things to do

8. Identify the organ on page 47. Discuss (a) why 8-foot pipes are not all 8 feet, (b) the visible pipe arrangement, (c) organ- playing difficulties, (d) why many organ subjects (and two-beater music) are zig-zags.
9. Write the notes sounded when an organist plays G below middle C using 16′, and 2′ stops.
10. Combine the four rhythms of bars 25–6 as ostinati.
11. Combine the following sequential 'jig' parts.
12. Play 'BACH' on any instruments.

10 FOOD FOR THOUGHT

Binary and ternary form

Things to do

1. Distribute melody copies of song/hymn books. Find tunes where the same phrase or part of a phrase occurs twice in succession, is used in a sequence or is repeated later. Any repetition need not be exact. If there is no sign of this, you may at least find rhythms that are repeated.
2. Sing the song on page 7. Discuss the phrase repetition. Now sing it making all four phrases exactly the same as the first. Does this spoil it?
3. Sing the song on page 12. Discuss (a) any sequence(s), (b) whether the final phrase is two or four bars long.
4. Sing the first song on page 13. Discuss (a) any immediate repetition of single bars, (b) the return to earlier music in the last four bars.

Find two reasons why this return needs to be modified. Now hear the song played with an exact repetition of the first four bars at the end.
5. Sing the song on page 38. Find inexact phrase repetition.
6. Turn to the minuet on page 43. Apart from the repetition of each half, is there any other phrase repetition? Find one- and two-bar sequences.
7. Look at the chorale on page 46. Identify (a) all repeated phrases/sections (written out or otherwise), (b) a near-sequence.

You have now discovered the importance of repetition in music. As each type of repetition is mentioned, look up the example indicated.

Whole sections
can be repeated:
(Minuet, page 43)

or just one phrase:
(Song, page 38, bars 1–2, 2–4)

or one bar:

Minuet
(page 43,
bars 1, 2)

There can also be:

Any repetition
can be exact:
(Song, page 7, bars 1–4, 5–8)

a later return
to earlier music
(1st chorale, page 46, bars 12–16, 32–6)

or changed slightly in pitch
(Minuet, page 29, bars 1–8, 1st/2nd tunes)

or played at a different pitch:
(Song, page 12, bars 1–2, 3–4)

often to end on doh

in a sequence

or changed in rhythm
(Song, page 13, bars 1–2, 13–14)

perhaps to suit different words

Very short tunes often just have rhythms repeated:
(Song, page 22, bars 1, 8)

Repetition is important in other arts as well. Without it, nothing would match!

But repetition must not be overdone. It is just as bad to have everything exactly the same:

Good building designs—and good musical 'recipes'—must balance repetition and contrast:

Musical design is called FORM. You have just seen the different ways repetition can be used in short pieces. You will be able to fit most short pieces into one of the following designs:

BINARY FORM has two sections

One or more phrases   One or more phrases

Each 'half' could be repeated

like bread and jam

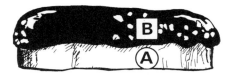

With some very short binary tunes
(see page 53, B can be very similar to A)

TERNARY FORM has three sections

One or more phrases   One or more phrases

Remember, the return of A may not be written
out. D.C. or D.S. may be used instead. The
end is then shown by *fine* or ⌢.

like a sandwich

B sections often contain musical
'crumbs' from A

Repetition plays an even bigger part in longer forms. For example, think
of what happens in Variations, Ground Basses and Fugues.

In your notebook

(i)(Copy, unjumbling the words)
Musical form usually involves *I norti pete.*
Brainy form is in two parts (AB) and *enry rat*
form in three parts (ABA).

D.C. or *Ada cop* tells a performer to return
to the beginning. D.S. or *sad no leg* indicates
a return to 𝄋 . The end of the piece is then
at *nife.*

Things to do

8. The songs and pieces on pages 12, 13, 29, 33, 38 and 43 are all in binary
or ternary form. Work out which, and also write down the bar numbers of
each A and B section.
9. Here are binary and ternary rhythm plans:

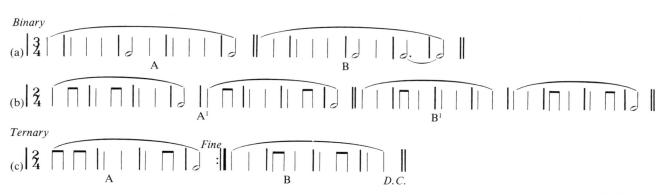

Divide into two groups (A and B) and clap or play the rhythms on contrasted percussion.
10. Now compose real tunes using these rhythm plans. Use these notes of the C pentatonic scale:

(i) End your tune on the home note (C):
(ii) If in binary form, do not end section A on the home note.
(iii) If in ternary form, section A may end on the home note. When it does not, modify it at the end. Jump only, 3rds, 4ths and 6ths. Otherwise, the five given notes may be used in any order. Vote for the best as each is played to you. Award a bonus as in 13 of Chapter 6.

Tempo terms

Composers usually like to tell performers how their music is to be played. They indicate at the beginning—and when any change is required:
(a) The dynamics
   pp p mp mf f ff cresc. or <decresc./dim. or>
(b) *The tempo* (also usually in Italian)
   largo, lento, adagio (*pron.* adarsyio)—slowly; andante (*pron.* andantay)—walking speed; moderato (*pron.* modderarto)—moderate speed; allegretto, allegro (*pron.* al aygro)—quickly; presto/prestissimo—very fast/as fast as possible.
All these can be modified by the use of words such as: molto—much; (un) poco—a little; non troppo—not too (much): accel(erando)—get faster; rall(entando), rit (ardando)—get slower; a tempo—original speed.

Things to do

11. The above dynamics are abbreviations of Italian words. Write these words and give each meaning. Why do conjurers say 'hey presto'? Why is Italian still the chief musical language?
12. Add dynamic and tempo markings to your compositions. Also indicate the instrument on which you will play it. Now practise it before taking your turn to play the piece to the class.
13. Design your own binary or ternary rhythm plan as above. Turn it into a tune as before.
14. Now see if you can improvise a tune using one of the rhythm plans. Play on the recorder or a class instrument with the unwanted bars subtracted. Either play straight away or work something out. Why will ternary plans require a good memory?

15. A four-bar 'question' phrase will be played or sung to you using just the above notes.
(a) All sing an 'answer' to 'la' simultaneously.
(b) Take turns at playing an 'answer' as in 14. Later, pairs of pupils could play 'questions' and 'answers' to each other. In all these activities remember 10(i) and (ii). 'Answers' not ending on the home note will sound more like further 'questions'.
16. Write down four-bar phrases played to you. Only duple time and crotchets and minims will be used. Both the notes and intervals used will gradually increase:
(a) CD, CDE stepping only, then with interval of 3rd.
(b) CDEG stepping only, then with 3rd, 5th.
(c) CDEGA as above.

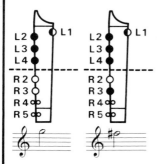

The next two recorder notes are upper 8ves of ones you can play already. Apart from being pinched, their fingering is identical, or very nearly so, to the lower notes.
   First practise changing between the two 8ves. Next, practise playing the scale of G major up and down at first largo, then moderato, and finally prestissimo!
   Now (a) repeat 14 and 15 of Chapter 6, playing the first part of the tune on the recorder, (b) playing the following:

Another cowboy song: **'The Streets of Laredo'**

A song from Hungary: 'Come and Sing Together'

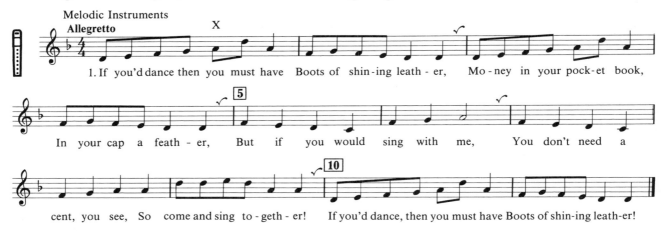

Melodic Instruments
Allegretto

1. If you'd dance then you must have Boots of shin-ing leath-er, Mo-ney in your pock-et book,

In your cap a feath-er, But if you would sing with me, You don't need a

cent, you see, So come and sing to-geth-er! If you'd dance, then you must have Boots of shin-ing leath-er!

Things to do

17. Clap and count the rhythm of each song (at the indicated tempi) before hearing it played.
18. When you can perform the above songs and accompaniments, discuss (a) repeated phrases, (b) which song is in binary, and which in ternary form, (c) the size of the 'crumbs' in the B sec-

tion of the binary song, (d) how performers can be counted in at the start of each.
19. Write out the A/B plan of each song, giving the bar numbers of each section.
20. Perform 'Come and Sing Together' as a round with a delay of half a bar (X). Recorders could play on their own or mix with the singers.

---

11   IT STRIKES A CHORD

Baroque dances

The dance movements from Baroque suites are always in binary form. You will usually find 'crumbs' from A in the B sections. For example,
(a) Repetition of rhythms;
(b) A similar opening, but at a different pitch or upside down (inverted);
(c) A similar ending, but at a different pitch.

(a) Listen to dances from Handel's *Fireworks* or *Water Music* or suites by Bach or other late Baroque composers.
(i) Work out the time of each, identifying the dance if you can. Is there an opening anacrusis?
(ii) Notice if the A and B sections are repeated.
(iii) Notice any 'crumbs' from A in section B.

Things to do

1. Practise these rhythmic ostinati designed to accompany certain Baroque dances:

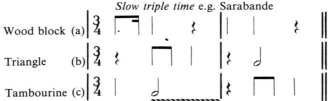

Slow triple time e.g. Sarabande

Wood block (a)

Triangle (b)

Tambourine (c)

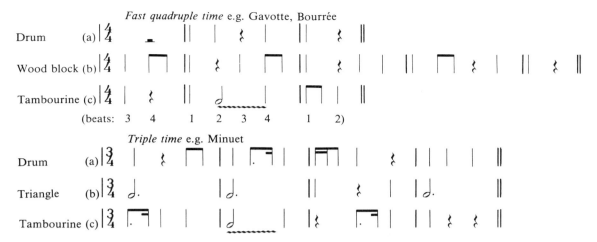

Fast quadruple time e.g. Gavotte, Bourrée

Drum (a)

Wood block (b)

Tambourine (c)

(beats: 3 4 1 2 3 4 1 2)

Triple time e.g. Minuet

Drum (a)

Triangle (b)

Tambourine (c)

2. Beat time as examples of the above dances are played. If there is an anacrusis do not start until beat one. Continue conducting when the volume is turned down. Are you still in time when the sound is turned up again?

3. Now take turns at adding the above ostinati to recordings of orchestral dances or keyboard dances played on the piano. Make sure all first beats fit together—even if there is an anacrusis in the music or ostinato.

Accidentals

The next piece is also in binary form. Its two 'halves' are very unequal. The music also changes 'tracks' or MODULATES at X.

The key signature tells us that the piece is in key F major. At X the music changes to the C major 'track'. This key does not require B flat. The naturals (♮) cancelling this can be seen in line 2. Later the music changes to yet other keys. Each one requires one or more notes different from the key signature to make the major scale pattern correct.

Any new #, b or ♮ cancelling the key signature is called an ACCIDENTAL. This is a very silly word: these changes are not unintentional—and they are certainly not accidents!

Accidentals have less powerful 'magic' than the key signature. The signature has power over the whole piece—unless it is changed or there are accidentals.

The power of an accidental over any note disappears at the end of the bar.

It is rather like the difference between railway or bus season tickets and single tickets. You have to buy another ticket (accidental) if you want to continue any changes in the next bar.

Binary pieces very often modulate at the end of the A section. A modulation here makes an effective contrast with the ending, which will always return to the original key. Even if short pieces do not modulate, the B section will rarely end on the home note (doh). Ternary pieces also often modulate in the middle B section.

The following solo sonata was written by Handel in Germany before he settled in England. As the set of sonatas was his first published work it is called OP(US) 1 (opus is the Latin for work):

55

Allegro from Sonata for treble recorder in F major, Op. 1, No. 11

Handel

(b) Listen to a recording of the above Allegro. Modern performances may be on the flute.

(i) Identify the solo instrument. If a treble recorder, any class players can compare their own instrument—and playing skill! Can you tell if the player breathes (⌢) in the long passages without a rest?

(ii) Name the accompanying continuo instrument(s). Now look at the music: Find (iii) 'crumbs' from A in B, (iv) two sequences in B. Listen to the recording again, this time carefully

following the recorder part. As it is fast (allegro), just follow the pitch shape up and down—as if it were a graph. Can you hear the modulation effects at each new accidental?

Finally, follow the continuo part, counting quadruple time. Notice that the bass is usually more interesting (and most easily heard) when the recorder part has longer notes or a rest.

Movements like this without a title can be referred to by their tempo name. Have you ever heard the famous piece usually just called

56

'Handel's *Largo*'? Discuss why this title is rather silly.
(c) Hear recorder solo or consort music by present-day composers. The Baroque period saw the end of recorder music—until the recent revival of interest.

Things to do

4. List the accidentals other than B♮ used in the above music (bass and treble staves). Discuss why we say, e.g., F sharp and place the sharp after the letter (F#) yet write the # *before* the note in music (sharp F).
5. Write down the last notes (both staves) of each section. This will help you find what is unusual about the Bach Minuet on page 29.
6. Look at the performers' names and any pictures on the record sleeve. Do you know of any other famous recorder players? Have you heard them?

In your notebook

(i) (Copy, unjumbling the words)
Change of key is called *dual motion*. The new notes required are shown by *dial accents*. These lose their power in the next *rab*.

Long works

This Allegro is the fourth and last movement of the sonata. Notice how much longer it is than the pieces you have composed. In most binary and ternary pieces the simple meals of bread and jam or a sandwich are made more filling.

Really long works like sonatas, suites and concertos, usually have several movements, each in binary or some other form. Church music and operas also divide up into different sections (or numbers).

Solo arias in Baroque oratorios and operas are usually in ternary (*da capo*) form. In these, singers are often able to show off in the runs of notes sung to just one syllable (COLORATURA). Do you remember examples of this in 'Rule Britannia'? They also often add extra ornamentation of their own in the repeat of the A section. Any important accompanying part for a solo instrument is called an OBBLIGATO.

(d) Listen to the aria 'O ruddier than the cherry' and its preceding recitative from Handel's opera *Acis and Galatea*. The giant Polyphemus is describing the beauties of Galatea—although his intentions are not as honourable as they sound! The obbligato on a special small recorder (sopranino) makes the giant look silly. Some performances use the descant recorder/flute.
(i) Identify the voice and obbligato instrument.
   In the recitative, notice (ii) the coloratura on 'rage', (iii) the low notes for 'capacious mouth'.
   In the aria, notice (iv) more coloratura on 'merry' in section A and 'lustre' in section B, (v), where the recorder is silent, (vi) whether the music/performance of the repeated A section is unchanged.
(e) Listen to Handel's Concerto, Op. 3, No. 6. In both movements, notice:
(i) The opening ritornello played by the full orchestra (*ripieno*) and the number of times it returns.
(ii) Which instrument(s) play the solo (concertino) sections
(iii) Sequences. Can you guess when they start?
(iv) Any obvious modulations.
   Finally, discuss what Op. 3, No. 6 means.

Life was generally more leisurely in the eighteenth century. People were quite prepared to listen to concertos like the following during the *intervals* of Handel's operas and oratorios!

The repeating ground bass, much used by Purcell, is also found in Bach and Handel. When instrumental variations are written above it the form is called a PASSACAGLIA (pronounced 'pass er carlia'). The following example is extra special. Throughout the movement, the bass is also played an 8ve higher by the other strings:

(f) First follow the music as the above ten opening bars are played. Do you consider the tempo 'walking pace' (*andante*)? Were all the parts played staccato? After this opening, every two bars of music is repeated until near the end.

Follow as before and then count four two-bar sections, each repeated. This will bring you to X above. Continue counting two-bar sections after this second extract. How many more are played twice/once? Can you guess when it is going to end? Now discuss (i) how Handel created variety and interest despite the unchanging string repetitions, (ii) a similarity with Bach's Air on page 33.

58

Chords and harmony

Handel achieved variety and contrast by:
Changes in dynamics
Contrast between the staccato and unvaried string quavers and the legato organ part.
A different organ rhythm/melody in every two-bar variation.
Modulation at X and later. (See the accidentals.)

There is also the contrast between single notes (and their 8ves) in bars 1–4 and note mixtures from bar 5 onwards. Just imagine the string 8ves repeated all those times without any other notes!

Note mixtures are called CHORDS.

In bars 5–10, and for much of the piece, only two notes are mixed at a time. Chords of just one interval mixture are unusual. The more usual chords of three or more different notes first occur at X, and then in the final two bars. The figures under the continuo part are a Baroque code—a musical shorthand indicating the chords to be played by any continuo keyboard player.

It is not just the chord mixture itself that is pleasant to hear. It is also pleasant to hear the mixtures changing (HARMONY). At X the pile of notes making each mixture is quite clear. It is even more clear in music like hymns and chorales where all the parts tend to move in the same rhythm:

With contrapuntal music like a fugue, the harmony is less clear. Yet, wherever you slice the 'sausages' you will get a chord:

Notice that the melody and bass (part) are just the top and bottom of each pile—and are also themselves part of each chord. In many ways the bass is as important as the melody.

Now look at the first two melody notes of the National Anthem. Although the same, they are HARMONISED differently.

Things to do

7. Listen to the above opening of the National Anthem (a) complete, (b) with each part omitted in turn. Which part(s) is (i) most clearly heard, (ii) most missed? Discuss why it is appropriate that bass is pronounced 'base'.

Now follow the music as each part is played in turn. Learn the given alto part and sing it as all the parts are played. Any broken voices can also learn the bass and/or tenor parts. Now sing as many parts as possible together.

Finally, listen to each part of the above Bach extract played slowly, separately and then together.

8. Listen to the opening of the National Anthem (a) played as written, (b) without a change of chord on 'save'. Which do you prefer?

9. Write down the different letters used in the National Anthem's first chord. Each simultaneously play one of them on any instrument. Repeat, playing one of the other notes or at a different 8ve. Discuss: (a) Why changing the order of the notes in a chord pile or having 'second helpings' at other 8ves does not change the chord's 'flavour'; (b) Other meaning(s) of the word 'harmony'.

10. Repeat 10 using the other three chord 'slices' above. Which two make the same mixture?

11. Turn to the Bach Minuet on page 29. In which bars are there chords of more than two notes? Now turn to the sonata on page 56. Here

the chords also look two-part. Why is this untrue?

In your notebook

(ii) (Copy, completing the words)
A mixture of different notes is called a ch____.
Its t____ note is the easiest to hear and sing.
The various mixtures used in a piece is the h____.

(g) Listen to bars 19–22 of the Handel passa-caglia again (page 58). Hear the effect of the sudden full chords at X and the following chord changes and modulations.

(h) Listen to the first movement below. The four violin concertos of Vivaldi's *Seasons* are full of word-painting. They are also full of sequences and the sort of music that suits the violin family—repeated note and alternating note tremolos. See if you can guess how each sequence is going to continue. Follow these sections:
(i) The above opening chord build-up (shivering in the snow). Identify any keyboard continuo.
(ii) Soloist—fast notes (wind whistling) interrupted twice by the orchestra;
(iii) *Tutti*—with interesting chord changes;
(iv) *Tutti*—tremolo patterns in sequence (running and foot-stamping);
(v) Soloist and continuo—long fast passage;
(vi) *Tutti*—quick repeated notes (winds) alternating four times with the soloist;
(vii) Similar to the beginning, followed by soloist rising sequence;
(viii) Soloist—repeated notes (teeth chattering);
(ix) *Tutti*—similar to (iv).

(a) What do the Italian words mean in the above extract? Finally (b) discuss Vivaldi's attempts at word-painting and (c) why repeated notes and tremolos suit the violin family.

Opening of 'Winter' from *The Seasons*:   **Vivaldi**

Aggicciato tremar trà neri algento

[score excerpt: Allegro non molto — 1st Violins, 2nd Violins, Violas, Cello/Bass Continuo]

Minor keys

You would hardly expect a piece about winter to be light-hearted. Serious or sad music is often not written in a major key. Instead, a different and less happy track of notes called a MINOR SCALE is used. A MINOR KEY can make both melody and chords more sad. However, minor does not mean less important than major! Composers can also modulate between major and minor keys in the same piece.

Things to do

13. The Handel Concerto (page 58) modulates to various minor and major keys after X. Which new #, b, and ♮ are required in these four bars?
14. Listen to minor scales played on the piano. Now hear 'Three Blind Mice' and the National Anthem played in a minor key. Also try singing them. Finally, compare the following minor key fugue subject played as written and then in its major key version.
15. Identify (a) scales, (b) tunes as major/minor.
16. Sing the first A section of the minor key song on page 54 as a canon from X. Repeat in its major key version.
17. Use two beaters to play a Bach fugue subject on a class instrument.

The following work is also in a minor key. It is also famous for its chords. A TOCCATA is a piece designed to show off a player's skill. Many fugues have another movement to go before them or are part of a long choral work. Notice the zig-zag subject:

Fugue subject from Toccata and Fugue in D Minor: Bach

 (i) Listen to the above work. In the Toccata, notice the fast showy notes, the impressive chords and the short pedal solo near the end. In the Fugue, notice the appearances of the above subject, any Baroque echo effects between different manuals and the final toccata-like section at the end when the contrapuntal fugue 'conversation' has finished. Listen for the surprise chord at the beginning of this, modulations after a fast passage and the famous series of chords at the very end—especially the bass. Try to tell when the final one is coming.

(j) Listen to a modern pop or synthesiser version of this work. Compare with the organ version. Turn the volume on and off to appreciate how regular Baroque motor rhythms are.

Messiah was written by Handel in England. The three-hour oratorio only took three weeks to write. No wonder his music manuscript is untidy! Is the notation up-to-date?

The sister of Dr Arne ('Rule, Britannia') sang the contralto solos for him. The movement alternates between plain chord sections and little fugues (FUGATI or FUGATOS) on different subjects—rather like a loud madrigal. The same words are always sung to each theme:

Themes from the Hallelujah Chorus (*Messiah*): Handel

(k) When you have followed the above theme, played on the piano, listen to a recording of the chorus. Notice:

(i) Theme A repeated—all parts together.
(ii) Theme B—all parts in unison/octaves, followed by more hallelujahs. Repeated. Put up your hand when you hear the trumpets.
(iii) Theme B in counterpoint with the hallelujahs.
(iv) A quiet section with simple chords. What words are sung?
(v) A fugato on C. Note the order of voices.
(vi) 'King of Kings', etc. sung by the sopranos, mostly on one note, accompanied by hallelujahs. Repeated, gradually, getting higher.
(vii) Another fugato on theme C mixed with 'King of Kings', etc.

(viii) Final hallelujahs.
(l) Listen to pop music with interesting harmony.
(m) Listen to modern experimental music with unusual chords. Remember musical fashions can change!

Assignments

(A) Find the names of (a) famous present-day cathedral or concert organists, (b) churches and halls with famous organs. Record sleeves, including those used for this chapter and the *Radio Times* can help you.
(B) List Bach, Handel and Vivaldi works appearing in one copy of the *Radio Times*.

12   THE CLASSICAL PERIOD

New musical styles were spreading well before Bach and Handel wrote their last works. For example, Bach's two most famous composer sons, Carl Philipp Emanuel and Johann Christian, were writing pieces very different from their father's. If you consider your parents old-fashioned, so did they!

The new styles developed into what we now call CLASSICAL. Unfortunately, this word is much used today. The best examples of anything from books to tennis strokes and football games are said to have 'classical' style or be 'classics'. It is even more confusing when so-called 'serious' music from all periods is called 'classical'. Classical is also used to describe the ancient civilisations of Greece and Rome.

The true Classical period of music stretches from about 1750 to the early 1800s. It refers just to a particular musical fashion—a style which can be compared with the beautiful forms of classical architecture.

Although some of the greatest music was written at this time, 'classical' is no guarantee of quality. Inferior music can be written in any style.

Classical style

You will find Classical music very different from the music of the Baroque. Instead of an unchanging rhythmic 'engine' there can be 'changes of gear' and even sudden stops. The music is much more clearly divided up into phrases. There is usually less counterpoint and the melody is more likely to be in the top part. As a result, the accompanying parts and the

bass are often less interesting to play than in Baroque music. Changes of key also now become particularly important.

The orchestra now began to settle down into the grouping of strings, woodwind, brass and percussion that is still normal today. With all these instruments available to help play the chords, a continuo keyboard was no longer necessary. As this player had previously con-

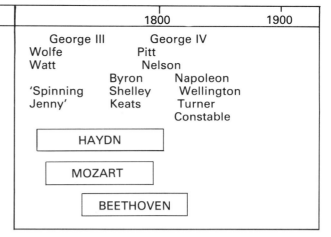

George III   George IV
Wolfe   Pitt
Watt   Nelson
    Byron   Napoleon
'Spinning   Shelley   Wellington
Jenny'   Keats   Turner
    Constable

HAYDN

MOZART

BEETHOVEN

trolled the performance, the LEADER of the first violins now had to 'conduct' the music.

At the end of the period, proper conductors with batons appeared on the scene. In any case, the harpsichord had at last been replaced by the piano. Think about why it was first called a FORTEPIANO (or PIANOFORTE).

Classical works

New important instrumental works include the SYMPHONY for full orchestra, the (STRING) QUARTET, the concerto for soloist(s) and orchestra and the sonata for solo piano or other instrument plus piano. Both the concerto and the sonata were quite different from the Baroque types.

Opera remained popular, but the comparatively little church music written was more suitable for concert performance than for use in worship. However, it was the new symphonies and concertos that were usually played at the public concerts. CHAMBER MUSIC, such as the quartet and music for other small ensembles, was more often played to small private audiences. The public taste was always for something new. This is why so many works were written during this period. They would not have wanted to listen to Bach or Handel—or even last year's symphony! In this, their attitude was very similar to today's treatment of pop music. Oddly enough, today's concert audiences usually prefer music from previous periods. Germany, and particularly what we now call Austria, was now unchallenged at the top of the composers' league. Vienna became the musical capital.

The Burgtheater in Vienna. Many of the works of Beethoven and Mozart were first performed here

63

Franz Joseph Haydn

Haydn was the son of a humble wheelwright. He was born (on April Fool's Day) in a village on the Austrian–Hungarian border in 1732. He made rapid musical progress and when eight was sent to be educated as a chorister in St Stephen's Cathedral in Vienna. His younger brother Michael, who also became a composer, joined him there later. When Joseph's voice broke he had to leave and make his own living.

Soon, his talents for playing and composing enabled him to make a respectable living. In 1761 he entered the service of the royal Esterházy family. Here, in a magnificent new palace, and as director of a large establishment of players and singers he was able to develop the Classical symphony and quartet. Late in life, he was allowed to make two important visits to London. He died in Vienna in 1809.

Wolfgang Amadeus Mozart

Mozart was born in a comparatively prosperous town house in Salzburg in 1756. His father, Leopold, was a composer and violinist employed by the local archbishop. Of his seven children, only two survived—Wolfgang, possibly the world's greatest musical infant prodigy, and a talented sister. At five Wolfgang was already composing, and his ambitious father took the children on several playing tours. They were shown off in Vienna, Paris and London, playing to many famous people, including Louis XV and our own King George III.

64

The Father of this Miracle, being obliged by Desire of several Ladies and Gentlemen, to postpone, for a very short time, his Departure from England, will give an Opportunity to hear this little Composer and his Sister, whose Musical knowledge wants not Apology. Performs every day in the Week, from Twelve to Three o'Clock in the Great Room, at the Swan and Hoop, Cornhill. Admittance 2/6 each person.

The two children will play also together with four hands upon the same Harpsichord, without seeing the Keys.

A London newspaper advertisement in 1765

During a year in London, Wolfgang met Johann Christian Bach, who had settled in England.

Back in Salzburg, Wolfgang was forced to leave his job with the archbishop. Later, after several European tours, he settled in Vienna, becoming a great friend of Haydn. Mozart died a pauper in 1791.

Ludwig van Beethoven

The son of an unimportant musician, Beethoven was born in the German town of Bonn in 1770. He met and impressed Haydn and Mozart in his youth and eventually settled in Vienna. He remained independent, not prepared to be treated like a servant—as were Haydn and Mozart. Deafness prevented his hearing his last great works. He died in 1827.

 (a) Hear short Classical extracts. Compare the 'fingerprints' with those of the Baroque.

In your notebook

(i) Describe the style of Classical music.
(ii) Briefly write the life stories of the above composers. Show their similarities/differences.

Assignments

(A) Write one or two sentences about all the non-musicians on the above chart.
(B) Collect material associated with Haydn, Mozart and Beethoven. Mount in your notebook.

13   MANY HAPPY RETURNS

Triplets

What were you doing when you were five? On the next page is a piece for early piano or harpsichord written by Mozart at that age! The K stands for Koechel, the man who catalogued Mozart's music in order of composition.

Things to do

1. Listen to this piece on the piano. Discuss:
(a) What is meant by prodigy;
(b) Other families of composers in history;
(c) If any class pianists have played this piece or others by Haydn, Mozart or Beethoven.
2. Write out the newspaper notice on page 64 in your own words.
3. Clap the RH rhythm of bars 1–4. Now follow the music again, identifying the bar number each time the playing stops. As bars 13–15 are a sequence, you can write out the missing bar.
4(a) What do you notice about the rhythm of each four-bar phrase?
(b) Count the returns of the first phrase.
(c) Is the form binary, ternary or a mixture?
(d) In which bar is there a modulation? Name all the accidentals required.
(e) The last two phrases have the same melody. Why do their endings have different effects?

Listen to the piece again. Notice the effect of (a) the modulation in bar 9, (b) the different LH in bars 20 and 24.

Discuss the effect when the last two phrases both end(i) as in bar 20, (ii) as in bar 24.
5. Clap the rhythm of bar 7 as it is played. What seems wrong with the note values used on the first beat?

When the beats are dotted, 'walk'

they divide into thirds
(not halves) 'gal - lop - ing'

Sometimes, the same effect is required with undotted beats. The composer then cheats and writes three TRIPLET quavers where there is only room for two proper quavers:
The ₃ may be omitted in repeated triplets.

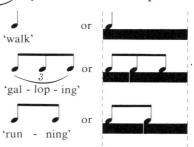

'walk'

'gal - lop - ing'

'run - ning'

Things to do

6. Clap crotchets, saying 'walk', etc. At a signal change to quavers ('running') and then triplets ('galloping'). Now combine at the same beat tempo, changing at each signal:

Discuss whether triplet quavers are (a) longer, (b) faster than proper quavers.
7. (i) Practise clapping the RH rhythm of bars 1–8 of the Mozart Minuet. (ii) Clap and say the note values of 5(a), (b) and (c) in immediate succession. Repeat (i) saying rhythm words.
8. Add the parts to the Minuet. If melodicas play the triplets, tongue (not finger) the repeated notes. Also, position doh and sing bars 1–8 of the 3rds to solfa as well.
9. Clap the Minuet's LH rhythm as the RH is played. Then clap the RH against the LH.
10. Compose and play a minuet using Mozart's phase plan (including the repetition). Choose note values from those he used, ending each phrase with a dotted minim. Use C pentatonic notes for repeating phrase A and G pentatonic notes for other phrases. Avoid jumps greater than a 5th. End on C.

Melodic/Class Instruments [all 3rds, incl. 3rd, 4th, 5th jumps] [introducing B♭]

Unpitched Percussion

Rondo

Although only the first part of A returns at the end, Mozart's Minuet is more like ternary form than anything else. Most Classical works have several movements.

Symphonies, quartets, sonatas and music for other ensembles usually have the same general four-movement plan:

1st movement—the most important, often quite fast
2nd movement—slow and melodic
3rd movement—a MINUET and TRIO (a quieter second minuet, or one for fewer instruments)
4th movement—fast

Concertos usually omit the minuet movement.

However, names such as symphony, concerto, quartet or sonata are not really forms. They refer instead to the ensemble or instrument for which the music is written.

Most movements have longer and more complicated forms than binary or ternary. But longer plans can cause problems. Music without any repetition would be unfriendly. We like to welcome back good tunes. But there must not be too much unvaried repetition (see page 50).

A form particularly used for the last movement of Classical concertos is called RONDO. The main rondo theme keeps coming back—like the Purcell tune (page 11).
And like the bread in a double-decker sandwich: Usually, it is even more of a mouthful:

Sometimes, certain of the 'sandwich fillings' also reappear later—as in the work below.

The Classical concerto is very different in style from the Baroque types. But it is still based on a contrast between the solo instrument(s) and the orchestra. The piano has always been the most popular instrument used. Most concertos have solo spots called CADENZAS. During a long orchestral pause

(⌢) the soloist often plays or improvises 'showy' variations on previous music.

The son of Bach who settled in London—Johann Christian—wrote some of the first piano concertos. Mozart met him during his year in England. He copied out some of his sonatas, later arranging them for piano and orchestra. Although the music was the same, they had to be called concertos! Before music colleges, copying out other people's music was one way of learning how to compose.

When older, Mozart wrote many beautiful concertos of his own. The following rondo theme is from the last movement—or FINALE ('finarlay') of one of them. Notice staccato dots and another use for the slur (reminding a performer to play legato).

(a) Hear any piano concerto movement by J. C. Bach. If on a fortepiano, compare the sound of harpsichord and modern piano.
(b) First hear the following theme played on the piano. Notice (a) the many large jumps, (b) the contrast between staccato and legato playing. Translate the Italian tempo words.
Now follow each 'slice of bread' (A), or its variation, as indicated below. The contrasting fillings between the slices are not given:
A—*tutti*, *p* then *f*;
A—end of previous *tutti*, then solo followed by violins decorated by piano;
A—shortened version on violins quickly followed by violas and then bass part in imitation;
A—two decorated versions on piano/violins and then *tutti*;
A—shortened version on strings with piano scales, repeated after short gap;
A—piano with jumping 8ves, then strings/oboe.

Now listen to alternating phrases between piano and orchestra, modulations and a pause on a loud chord. The soloist's cadenza immediately follows. Try to guess when it is going to end. In the final section Mozart varies the theme by using thirds of a beat. To save writing triplets on every beat, Mozart changes the time signature to 6/8. Finally, discuss
(i) Why the piano is more popular for concertos than stringed instruments;
(ii) Similarities between rondo and ritornello.

Rondo theme from 3rd movement of Piano Concerto, K.449:   **Mozart**

In your notebook

In your notebook

(i) In your own words, briefly explain the following: Symphony, Concerto, Quartet, Sonata. Describe the Classical four-movement plan.

Orchestral woodwind instruments

The new clarinet completed the basic orchestral (wood)wind section. The CROSS-BLOWN flute, not the gentle recorder (FIPPLE/WHISTLE flute) now had to be used:

Flute   Clarinet   Oboe   Bassoon

Each instrument's COMPASS divides into distinctive high/low REGISTERS (corresponding to pinched/unpinched recorder notes). The difference in TIMBRE (*pron.* tambrer) between instruments is partly due to the way the vibrations are started:

Single reed   Double reed   Double reed in a CROOK

Bassoons are usually referred to by their Italian name of fagotti (Fg). The long tube doubled back on itself resembles a bunch of sticks (faggots).

Piccolo   Bass clarinet   Cor anglais   Double bassoon

Later composers also sometimes introduced new instruments. For example, the saxophone appeared in the nineteenth century. Many sizes of this single-reed instrument have since been used in all kinds of music.

Saxophone

Things to do

11. Watch any wind players (including recorders) demonstrate (a) 'blowing' notes, (b) fingering, (c) different registers. Carefully examine reeds, keys, etc. Underneath their 'plumbing', wind instruments are just simple tubes with holes—like the recorder. Discuss:
(d) How and where the vibrations occur;
(e) Why pressing a key changes the pitch;
(f) Why keys are necessary;
(g) What determines the lowest pitch;
(h) Why the bassoon's tube is doubled back and a crook is needed;
(i) Other instruments with bends or a crook;
(j) Which are the highest and lowest instruments shown opposite.
12. Experiment with your own single or double 'reeds' using silver paper, drinking straws. Play 'Old Paint' (page 38) on comb and paper.
13. See how tricky it is to play the flute. Blow across objects such as bottles and pen tops. See how many different ways you can whistle.
14. In groups, assemble or tune six bottles to 'blow' the notes required for 'Old Paint' (DEF GAB). The best 'blower' play to the class. Now compare the effect of hitting with a beater.
Hear woodwind demonstration recordings. (d) Identify the woodwind instruments as each is featured as a solo in different pieces. Translate 'cor anglais'. Why is it a silly name? (e) Hear music for woodwind ensemble. Identify prominent solos as they occur. (f) Hear the clarinet playing jazz. Suggest why the flute, oboe and bassoon are rarely used. (g) Hear the final rondo movement from Mozart's Clarinet Concerto, one of his last works.

Count the number of times the A theme appears, played by (i) the soloist, (ii) the orchestra.

Notice also (iii) two occasions when short imitations of A occur in the long 'fillings' (crumbs), (iv) the clarinet's registers.

68

In your notebook

(ii) (Copy, completing the words)
Four types of w____ instruments are regularly used in the orchestra:
The fl___, played by bl___ across a hole;
The cl___, which has a single r____ made from thin cane;
The ob____ and b____, which have double r____ very similar to flattened drinking straws.
The gentler r—— would never have been heard in the classical orchestra.
Players change p____ by changing the vibrating length of enclosed air. This is done by opening or closing h____ in the side of the tube using fingers or k____.

(iii) Illustrate (ii) by copying/tracing the given pictures.

Assignment

(A) Collect further material concerning wind instruments, and mount in your notebook. Include pictures and information on both instruments and present-day players.

14   THREE'S COMPANY

Variations

Tunes can also be repeated without contrasted 'fillings'—provided variations occur:
(a) The tune itself can be varied;
(b) The variations can just be in the accompaniment. It is rather like 'eating' the same tune with 'gravy', 'custard', etc.
(Remember the Handel Passacaglia.)
(c) The tune can be heard in a lower part. It is fun listening for 'buried treasure'.

In the following variation movement by Haydn the tune hardly changes. Instead the variation methods are (b) and (c). Many pieces, including this one, have extra music at the end to round things off. This is called the CODA. Even pop music can have a short coda. These 'tailpieces' might not seem important. But they give both balance and a good finish!

The theme of Haydn's variations was his answer to our own National Anthem. He had been impressed by 'God Save the King' during his two visits to London. In 1797, the elderly composer felt that a similar tune with patriotic words about his own Emperor was needed by his countrymen—under threat from Napoleon's invading armies. The tune was an immediate hit, so Haydn then used it again as the slow movement theme of this work.

The theme continued to have quite a history! Robert Newton, an English ex slave-trading sea captain during Haydn's earlier years, wrote hundreds of hymns after his conversion to Christianity. One of these, 'Glorious things of Thee are spoken', started to be sung to Haydn's tune in the nineteenth century.

During the second world war the Nazis used the same tune for a fierce nationalistic song.

Haydn wanted his theme to be played in a smooth singing style—CANTABILE. This is why the first six notes are to be played in one slow bow stroke. Notice that this gives yet one more use for the slur!

Some notes are to be accented.
Haydn uses *fz* SFORZANDO (*pron.* 'sfort zando') He could also have written *sf* or *fp* for the same effect.

The ∞ , ♪ and ♪ indicate different types of ornamentation for the first violin part. Neither Mozart nor Beethoven could match Haydn's output of over eighty quartets!

Second movement theme of Quartet in C major, Op. 76, No. 3   **Haydn**

 (a) First follow the first violin part as just the theme is played in a recording. Notice the smooth bowing, the accented chords and the way each type of ornament is played.

Is the theme of this variation movement binary or ternary? In which bar does the B section begin? Find all the double stops. Discuss how they are played.

Now listen to the whole movement. The theme is repeated four more times, once in each instrument.

Variation 1. Two violins only. Is the theme mainly above or below the continuous semi-quavers in the other part?

Variation 2. Four parts, which instrument has the theme?

Variation 3. Identify the instrument with the theme. Notice the other parts enter the accompanying musical conversation in turn. Which instrument comes in last? After this,

notice (i) modulations, with parts moving by semitones (chromatic), (ii) a scale joining the 8ve jump between the last two phrases of the theme.

Variation 4. The first violin has the theme again. Notice (iii) the effect of different harmony and modulations in the first phrase, (iv) all the parts jump an 8ve higher as the phrase is repeated this time, (v) the rising 8ve scale and the following modulations and semitones as in Variation 3, (vi) the final short four bar coda—especially the last two rich sustained chords.

Now discuss:
(vii) The main key of this movement. Why is the quartet described as being in key C?
(viii) Why there is not one of each member of the violin family in a string quartet;
(ix) Why chamber music is so called;
(x) Why this work is nicknamed the 'Emperor'.

70

Triads

Things to do

1. Sing the hymn that uses this tune. Watch any violinist play the theme. See how several notes are played on one bow stroke. Compare slurred bowing with separate strokes.

2. Work out the notes used in the chord at X. Now choose any one of them and mix them together simultaneously, using any instruments. Similarly treat the chords at Y and Z. Finally, hear the effect as the three chords are played in succession in all the orders possible.

3. Look at bars 1, 2, 5 and 6 where only the two violins are playing. What interval mixture is made each time?

The above Haydn extract, written out in open score, is full of beautiful chords. Here is chord 'Y' again, written on a reduced SHORT (or PIANO) SCORE:

From the bass, the notes used are C E G and E. The three different letters used can be arranged in a simple close pattern:

You would expect this chord mixture to sound pleasant. It consists of the pleasant interval of a 3rd, written twice as well as the bare 5th.

This three-note pattern is called a TRIAD. Each triad takes its name from its starting point,

or ROOT:

This is therefore the triad or chord of C. Triads (chords) can be built on any root. For example, chord 'Z', which consists of G D B G and B, can be arranged as this simple triad:

It is therefore the triad or chord of G

(The letters above the songs, etc., indicate the chords to be played by a guitar or other accompanying instruments.)

The notes of a triad can be arranged in any order the composer pleases. The root is often in the bass (and can be plucked on cello/bass open strings), but it need not be there. There can also be 'second helpings' or other octaves of any of the triad notes. For example, chord 'Z' has two Gs, two Bs and one D.

All these rearrangements or extras do not affect the basic 'flavour' of a chord, but they usually give it a richer sound.

(c) Listen to a modern folk/pop song that has interesting chord changes. Does it have a coda?

In your notebook

(i) Briefly explain what is meant by triad and root. Use the chord of C as your example.

Things to do

4. Hear the basic chord of C (a) played (as opposite), (b) in other arrangements and with 'second helpings'. Repeat with other chords. Finally, with eyes closed, put up your hand when a different chord is played.

5. Write out chords 'X' and 'Z' in short score as 'Y' above. At 'Z', although the double stopping makes five notes, why do you only have to write four?

6. Write out chord 'X' as a simple triad on the treble stave (not forgetting the sharp). Name its root. Explain why the triad pattern of two 3rds adds up to a 5th and not a 6th.

7. Now write out the chord at the beginning of bar 15 in short score. Is the root in the bass?

8. Copy and complete the following to make the chords of C and G. In both cases have two helpings of the root. Also write two notes on each stave as for chord 'Y' above:

C   G

Now listen to them played in succession on the piano. Notice that the same top (tune) note G fits both chords. Remember, the National Anthem also begins with two Gs and a change of harmony underneath. Before hearing it, are these the chords used?

9. Choose two letters one from each of the above chords. All play them in succession on any instruments, damping if necessary. Repeat, choosing different letters or different 8ves. Why is the basic chord flavour unchanged despite second helpings and 8ve changes?

10. Rewrite each of these letters at a different 8ve, without using leger lines:

Now, as many as possible take an instrument capable of playing the letters required—either at the correct 8ve as above or in your version, or at any 8ve on a class instrument. Simultaneously play each letter when directed. Spot 'odd men out'.

11. Repeat 10 replacing the 𝄞 with 𝄢 This will 'magically' change all the letters.

12. Turn to 'The Streets of Laredo' (page 53). Each take one chime bar or a bar of a shared instrument so that all the notes of the song are covered (at any 8ve). Play the tune slowly under a conductor. Hit (and damp) your bar when it comes in the tune. Repeat, changing bars. Also, see if you can play without a conductor.

13. First hear the following hidden tune played on the piano as written. Do you recognise it? Now play it as in 12, each with one of the notes required. First clap the rhythm at a slow tempo:

etc.

The above is a disguised version of the piece on page 66. It is also transposed from key F to key C. Write out the above opening as it should be played. The first note is correct.

Changing 8ves makes a tune sound odd—and also look very odd. But the 8ve family likeness should just about make it recognisable.

However, as you have discovered, changing 8ves or having 'second helpings' hardly affects a chord's basic flavour at all. This is why you can choose which chord notes to play in the accompaniment of the next song.

Things to do

14. Without looking at the music, hear the next song played through with just the opening chord as the accompaniment. Repeat, this time putting up your hand when you feel the chord should first change. Look at the music and suggest why a change is necessary at this point. Now hear it played with the correct accompaniment. Notice how effective the various chord changes are. In which bar does it modulate? The natural in bar 9 is not absolutely necessary. Why is it put in? Why is there a quaver missing in the last bar?

15. The chords required in the accompaniment are the triads of G(BD), A(C#E), C (EG) and D (F#A).

First write each of these out on the treble stave as simple triads. Next, choose (a) one chime bar and only play when required by the chord, (b) a different chime bar for each chord.

Now, looking at the music, accompany the tune played on the piano. Repeat or change chords as indicated. Later, use a chromatic class instrument/melodica/recorder instead to play your chosen chord note(s).

16. Accompany the singing of the song (and/or recorders playing the tune) with a group playing as in 15.

17. Practise the written accompanying parts. Listen particularly to the pleasant effect of the 3rds. Finally, add to 18.

18. Prepare for the next section by improvising a tune on 'The Stuttering Lovers' rhythm, playing any 'black' and 'white' notes on a Class Instrument. Just let yourself go. Don't stop to choose particular notes. Play singly and in twos/threes.

A folk song from Ireland: 'The Stuttering Lovers'

Experimental chords

Chords built from triads are not the only kind. Although all the composers mentioned so far have based their chords on triads, many in our century have experimented with other mixtures. Any mixture is a chord, however strange or clashing.

Things to do

18. About five pupils stand at the piano. All play any two notes simultaneously, holding the keys down. Listen to the unusual chord and then to the effect of the keys being raised in random order. Repeat with different pupils/notes.

19. All take any fading-note instrument. Play together and then listen to the effect as the bars are damped quietly in various sequences. For example, in alphabetical or seating order.

20. Use instruments as in 19. Take a playing card or a number and keep it a secret. Play together with eyes closed. Damp when your card or number is called. Listen carefully and point in the direction of each damper.

21. Again play your notes together. While they are still sounding, one of them will be played on the piano. Call out 'Bingo' if it matches yours (at any 8ve). Score + and − points.

22. Hear two sustained pitches. In which pattern are they stopped? Repeat with three pitches and similar diagrams on the board:

(a) ▬▬▬▬   (b) ▬▬   (c) ▬▬▬
    ▬▬▬▬   ▬▬▬▬   ▬▬▬

23. Identify which of two (or three) pitches played together rises/falls a semitone.
24. Play the following grids (pitches shown).
25. Repeat (b) without conductor. Each play at any tempo, with accel. and rit.

26. Choose an instrument and write a single part for it to fit grid (a). All play together. Repeat with (b) (on treble stave).
27. Compare new grids with your spacing, pitches, dynamics. Perform each in groups.

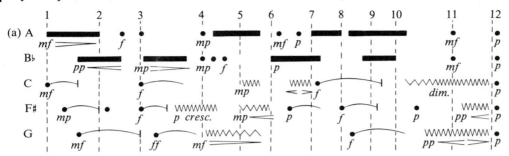

(b) (This requires a regular beat)

15 ENOUGH OF YOUR LIP?

Key D major

Haydn's two visits to London were triumphant successes. Here he directed performances of Symphonies 93–104! These *London* symphonies proved to be his last.

However, neither Mozart (forty-one symphonies) or Beethoven (nine) could match this output.

During Haydn's first London visit in 1791–2, he received news of the death of Mozart. It is believed that the music you are about to hear is Haydn's tribute to his great friend.

The main key of this symphony is E♭. This reminds us that scales may start from any 'black' flat or sharp as well as any 'white' natural.

For example, the major scale staircase from C becomes the major scale from C# when each step is raised by a half-tone 'carpet':

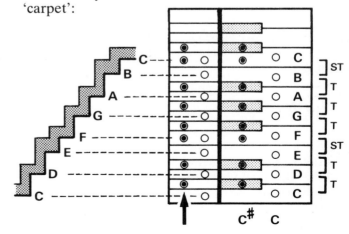

74

Both the 'staircase' and the keyboard show that the TTSTTTS interval pattern is unchanged when a 'carpet' raises all the steps by the same amount.

Raise them by another semitone:

and we get the scale of D major:

The key signature of D major gives the two sharps required:

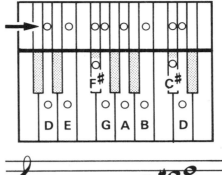

(a) First hear just the opening five notes of the slow movement of Haydn's 98th symphony in E♭. What famous tune does it remind you of? Now hear the complete movement. Count the number of times this phrase is used. Apart from appearing in one short musical conversation, it is always harmonised quite simply. Notice how its harmony is changed at its second appearance, and later. Finally, discuss whether you could say, 'My grandfather's grandfather's grandfather's grandfather met Haydn in London'.

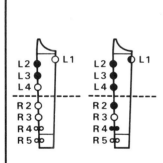

The next two recorder notes will enable you to play the scales of D and F major. Practise these scales when you can play the new notes. Compare the effect when you play these scales using only naturals. Now play 'Three Blind Mice' and 'The First Nowell' by ear in keys C, D, F and G major, starting from the third note of the scale in both cases.

See if you can echo short phrases played to you in one of the above keys. Play the scale first. You will be told the starting note. When you can copy stepping phrases, 3rd jumps will be introduced.

Notes can be joined more smoothly if they are tongued as one 'too'. Again a slur is used to show this:

Repeat 'The First Nowell' in keys C, D, F and G, joining the quavers at the beginning of each phrase in this way. Finally, play Haydn's theme (page 70) (slurring as for the violin bowing).

Things to do

1. Sketch a keyboard, e.g.

Continue the ○ to complete the scale of E♭ major. Also write each letter once as shown. Do the flats match the key signature on page 77? Similarly show one octave of the A major scale on another sketch. What have the scales in common? Now name the key modulated in bar 3 of 'Barbara Allen' and bar 8 of 'The Stuttering Lovers' (page 73).

2. Practise the parts before accompanying the next song sung and/or played. Repeat 'Stuttering Lovers' (page 73) with any recorders playing the Class Instruments parts.

A folk song from Britain: **'Barbara Allen'**

Embouchure

Woodwind instruments, like the keyboard, are chromatic and can play in all keys. The different notes required are made by opening and closing holes.

It is not so easy with brass instruments. They have no holes in the tube. They also have no reed or sharp edge to start the vibrations in the tube. Instead, the player makes the vibrations with his lips. Just blowing creates no vibrations and no musical sound—only a gale force wind!

Things to do

5. Carefully pass round any available brass instrument. Imagine the tube straightened out. Roughly how long would it be? See if you can get a note out of it. Blow a gentle 'raspberry' into the mouthpiece—as if you were getting rid of a hair from your lips. Do successful players get the same note?

6. Now see who can get more than one note without operating the instrument in any way. Any brass players can also demonstrate how many they can get.

7. Listen to any prepared pieces by brass players.

Even good players cannot get many notes from one length of tube. The higher and lower notes are obtained by progressively tightening and slackening the lips. The lips and the way the mouth is used is called the EMBOUCHURE (the embouchure of wind instrument players is also important, affecting both timbre and pitch).

Modern brass instruments therefore have the means to change the length of the tube. Each length gives the player another set of available notes. The trombone has an obvious way of changing length. The others have three valves controlling three diversions:

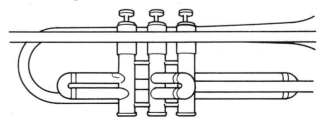

To play any particular note, the player
(a) Chooses the tube length required:
(b) Adjusts his embouchure.

Orchestral brass instruments

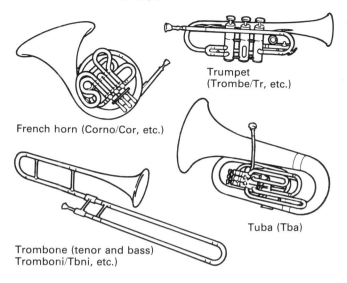

French horn (Corno/Cor, etc.)

Trumpet (Trombe/Tr, etc.)

Tuba (Tba)

Trombone (tenor and bass) Tromboni/Tbni, etc.

The cornet is very similar to the trumpet. Other modern brass instruments are also different sizes or modifications of the above. On scores, the Italian names are usually used.

Mozart wrote four Horn Concertos for a friend called Leutgeb who kept a cheese shop in Vienna. He had to cope with an instrument without valves—and Mozart's jokes. The composer wrote remarks such as 'poor swine' and 'thank God, here's the end' all over the scores. He even used four different coloured inks in the 4th concerto, just to confuse poor Leutgeb. The early 'natural' horn was certainly a problem. However, the few notes available could be increased by putting a hand inside the instrument's BELL and modifying each one. By Mozart's time, extra pieces of tubing (again called crooks) could be inserted. Leutgeb's crook for the following would have been chosen to suit key Eb. Valves, invented in the nineteenth century, made all brass instruments chromatic.

The Rondo theme from the finale of Mozart's Horn Concerto No. 4 in E^b, K 495

Allegro vivace

(b) During this Rondo, count the number of times the complete theme appears in the (i) horn, (ii) orchestra. Is there a cadenza?
(c) Hear recordings demonstrating brass instruments. Why are some Italian names misleading?
(d) Identify featured brass instruments.
(e) Listen to modern music for brass ensemble.
(f) Listen to the final variation movement of Mozart's *Sinfonia Concertante*, K. 297b—a sort of concerto for four instruments. The sixteen-bar binary theme has an extra eight bars 'coda'. First count the 24 quadruple bars of this theme. As you follow the ten variations (i) write down the instrument that first takes the lead in each one, (ii) notice that each 'coda' is much less varied and played by the full orchestra. At the end of Variation 10 there is a ritardando and a surprise chord. This leads into the coda proper. There is then an extra dotted beat variation. Finally, list the four solo instruments used.

In your notebook

(i) Under a suitable heading, list and illustrate the brass instruments given above.
(ii) Explain and illustrate how a valve works.

The harmonic series

The notes obtainable from just one tube always makes the same pattern of intervals—or HARMONIC SERIES. For example:

3rd — 6th harmonic
4th — 5th harmonic
5th — 4th harmonic
3rd harmonic
2nd harmonic
8ve — 1st harmonic or FUNDAMENTAL (not easily sounded)

Notice how the harmonics gradually get closer as they go up.
Notice also that the first six harmonics make the triad on its fundamental with 'second helpings':

Before the invention of valves, brass tunes could only step if they were very high. Such tunes therefore usually jumped around the lower harmonics. This explains why bugle calls, hunting calls and brass parts in Classical symphonies are alike.

'Come to the cook-house door, boys' etc.

Broken chords and arpeggios

Valveless instruments have to play tunes based on triad patterns. Mozart's horn rondo theme has the typical jumpy shape. However, most performances of it today are on modern valve horns.

Phrases built from the notes of chords have often been used by composers—and not just for brass instruments. See the fugue (page 48), sonata (page 56) and Minuet (page 66). This is why musicians practise various BROKEN CHORD patterns: e.g.

Those that go straight up (and down) are called ARPEGGIOS (pronounced 'ar pedge ee oes'):

Sometimes the broken chords are a continuous feature—as in the opening of Beethoven's Piano Sonata No. 14 in C# minor, Op. 27, No. 2:

(g) Listen to the above first movement. Notice (i) the effect of a minor key, (ii) the continuous broken chord triplet pattern. How could Beethoven have avoided using triplets? (iii) Phrases of louder, longer notes, each changing as the chords change. Later musicians have named this sonata the *Moonlight*. Do you think this is a good title?

Now hear the last movement! In which hand are the broken chord passages?

More often, the broken chords are a lower accompaniment—as in the Trio opening of Mozart's Symphony No. 39 in E♭, K. 543:

(h) Listen to the Minuet and Trio from Mozart's 39th Symphony. What movement would this be? Listen particularly to the first part of the trio. Identify the instrument(s) playing (i) the tune, (ii) the broken chord accompaniment in a low register. Now hear the movement again.

Each section of both Minuet and Trio is repeated. The Minuet is played again after the Trio, but without repeats. What is the form of the (iii) Minuet, (iv) Trio, (v) the whole movement?

Things to do

8. Turn to the sonata on page 56. What are the roots of the recorder broken chords in bars 1 and 9?
9. Watch any players of piano/orchestral instruments play different broken chords and arpeggios.
10. Repeat 6. Write each new note on a stave as it is sounded. Does the pattern match the harmonic series on page 77? Are the notes the same? Any recorder players can also demonstrate harmonics (a) by pinching, (b) by fingering the bottom note and deliberately overblowing. Now discuss (c) why recorder/brass wrong notes are often very wrong, (d) why many brass tunes are jumpy, (e) the number of

tube lengths obtainable using three valves, (f) why musicians practise scales and arpeggios.
11. Sing in three groups, listening to the final chord:

Repeat with a changed doh and then with r f l.
12. Sing the following, d m s tune as a round:

78

So, triads can also be built using singing names, e.g.:

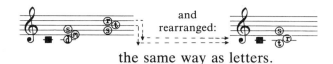

the same way as letters.

Here are these two chords as three stepping singing parts:

and arranged as a broken chord 'um pah' accompaniment:

Things to do

13. Practise parts (a) and then combine them as an accompaniment to 'One man went to mow' on the piano. Similarly treat parts (b).

14. Sing/play this stepping melody and broken chord accompaniment:

15. Improvise or write your own 'bugle calls' in quadruple time. Use this rearranged doh me soh triad in key C, broken in any way you like:

Choose four to put on the board. Practise singing each to solfa and then combine them in four groups.

16. When you wach a brass (or woodwind) player can you tell if the notes fingered are 'black' or 'white'?

17. Discuss all the musical and non-musical meanings of the word 'key'.

Assignments

(A) Collect material on brass instruments and present-day orchestral players. Mount in your notebook. Use record sleeves/magazines/programmes, etc.

(B) Write, comparing conditions and life generally in the Baroque and Classical periods. Let the 'Wheels of Fashion' in Chapters 5 and 12 help you.

Index

Capital letters indicate the first use of that technical term in the Series. Terms already introduced in Book 1 are not shown.